Philosophy Junk-Food
Wisdom from the MTV Generation
By David Schuster

Text Copyright © David Schuster, 2006
This text may not be reproduced or transmitted in any form or by any means in part or in whole without written permission from the author, all rights reserved

Art Copyright © Katherine Mills, 2006
The cover artwork may not be reproduced or transmitted in any form or by any means without written permission from the artist, all rights reserved

Printed in the United States of America

ISBN: 978-0-6151-3855-8

To my parents, Judy and Larry, my sister Rachel, my brother-in-law Scott and my muse Kate

"I'm still looking for these angels in the snow" - Brock Lindow of 36 Crazyfists

"How can you buy or sell the sky, the land? The Earth does not belong to Man, Man belongs to the Earth. All things are connected like the blood that unites us all. Man did not weave the web of life; he is merely a strand of it. Whatever he does to the web, he does to himself."

– **Chief Seattle**

Table of Contents

0. Introduction

1. Responsibility

2. Sex

3. Drugs

4. Rock and Roll

5. Love

6. Commitment

7. Ideas, Symbols and Sources

8. The Meaning of Life

9. Women and Men

10. Happiness and Sadness

11. A Partridge in a Pear Tree

Appendix. Suggested reading, watching and listening

Disclaimer

For anyone that actually cares to read this monstrosity, I feel I must qualify it. These are the random thoughts of someone that actually *chose* to study physics in college and graduate school. I leave you with this unsettling question about my sanity as you wade through this work. Basically, take what you read here with a grain of salt. Thank you.

P.S. – Throughout this work, if there is a neuter personal pronoun, I use the masculine form, i.e. he, him, his. To the best of my knowledge, this is the proper usage and does not indicate any kind of misogyny or support of a tyrannical patriarchal language scheme. So back off.

Introduction

Hello. My name is David Andrew Schuster. I'm a 24 year old, middle class, Jewish, white, male, graduate student. I am originally from Albuquerque, New Mexico. I have a Bachelor's degree in physics from the University of Arizona in Tucson, a Master's degree in physics from the University of Miami and, as of this printing, am pursuing a Ph.D in astrophysics at the University of Denver. Since you picked up this book to begin with, I'd have to say that your tastes in literature must tilt outside of the mainstream. After all, while it's incredibly unfashionable to be a white, middle class, male in these days and times; it's even more unfashionable to support one. We don't seem to be outwardly oppressed in any way, yet we've done more than our fair share of oppressing over the years. This seems to have made us very unpopular.

Due to the fact that I was born in 1981 and that I honestly didn't really know what the hell was going on outside of my own little existential bubble until at least 1995, I can say with some measure of certainty that I had absolutely nothing to do with the oppression of Native Americans, Blacks, Women, Puerto Ricans, starving Ethiopian children or anyone else there are liberation marches for. However, there are a great many people that believe me and all of my ilk are directly responsible for all the injustices perpetrated by our predecessors, and that we should be condemned to the wastebasket of history as a group of obsolete, static, quasi-evil and (most of all) uncool dinosaurs.

Before I begin a rebuttal to this statement, let me make it very clear that I'm not bitter at all. I realize that I couldn't choose to be born as I am any more than someone can choose to not be born with Down's Syndrome. It's a roll of the big genetic dice. Tall or short, genius or disabled, A cup or D cup it's all those damned kooky genes. That having been said, I'd like to say that I am definitely *not* responsible for any shit storm anyone reading this book has ever had to endure. EVER. I can give you my personal guarantee on that. It may surprise a lot of people out there but a lot of us guys actually do have feelings and, yes, they can be hurt. And I just want to use this opportunity to say, stop ragging on us! Perhaps the great pendulum of Karma is swinging back, but I'd like to think that maybe, just maybe, the human race as a whole is mature enough to realize that this kind of mindless posturing and finger-pointing is getting us nowhere, so why don't we just accept each other and go on? Little me, the eternal optimist.

I'm getting ahead of myself though. I really wanted to use this introduction to tell you what you can and can't expect from this little collection. What you can expect: *lots* of opinions, *lots* of opinions you don't agree with, *lots* of condemnations of popular icons i.e. the media, many television programs and many widely held beliefs (note: this piece is not meant to offend anyone, there will be times when I will talk in vast generalizations, keep in mind that anything I say is purely based on my own experiences and my unique interpretation thereof- please be patient). What you can't expect: flashy sound bites designed for the ADHD culture of America, unbiased analyses of issues from both sides and polite expression of said analyses.

I want to be clear about the purpose and nature of this book. It is a collection of essays illustrating my opinions on issues that I consider very important to our society and culture at this point in history. This piece is my catharsis- the one release valve for my tumultuous views about the world. In this crazy sensory overload that we call America, it's easy to drown in the constant, unebbing tide of stimulation. This piece provides a snapshot of how I felt at the time of this writing and at this place in my life. Take from it what you want, but I hope, no matter what you get out of it, that you enjoy yourself. As a final note, I'd simply like to say that I love life; it's always better than the alternative.

Responsibility

The word responsibility is a word that is indelibly associated with wisdom, age and maturity. I've been told that no one can ever truly be an adult without first knowing what responsibility is and understanding its importance. I agree with this statement to a certain degree. I don't know exactly what the spirit of this idea is, but I personally think that taking responsibility is a hell of a lot more important than some touchy-feely bullshit about "understanding responsibility." I understand that shooting heroin is unhealthy, but it's a much more significant fact that I choose not to do it.

There is a fundamental difference between "understanding" and "taking" responsibility. The former is a passive undertaking whereas the latter is an active undertaking. Our modern language and thinking has become so passive and euphemistic that it seems its purpose is to *avoid* making any kind of definitive statement. The distinction between our modern passive thought and active thought corresponds to "understanding" heroin's deleterious effects vs. making an active choice not to take heroin. Many people completely understand that heroin causes chronic death syndrome, but at the same time lack the audacity to make the choice not to take it.

The passive/active boundary is where I believe many of society's problems with responsibility lie. In the increasingly politically correct world we live in, it's more important to make a statement than to actually take action. We elect leaders who are charismatic and tell us exactly what we want to hear and then find ourselves complaining mid-term that they never get anything done. We watch plodding rallies supporting feminism/environmentalism/civil rights which ultimately achieve nothing. What scares me most is that we, as a culture, have begun to think that they do mean something. Cultivating this passive attitude is a very dangerous thing for our culture- perhaps most dangerous when applied to responsibility.

It has become "enough" to admit that a certain action was known to be wrong, but it was committed anyway. This has become analogous to taking responsibility for an action. I know that some of you are sitting at home right now and thinking "Well, yeah! That *is* taking responsibility!" I suppose in some very limited way, it is. However, (once again I am the optimist) I would *hope* that if someone can recognize an action is wrong before he commits it, it wouldn't be committed.

This is beside the point, however. The real difference between this pseudo-responsibility vs. real responsibility is the fact that now-a-days, pseudo-responsibility is an excuse for a wrong action. It's even worse when pseudo-responsibility is coupled with a shift of blame; this is the true travesty. "Well I knew killing my dog was bad, but my parents are so abusive to me, I didn't care." This kind of defense can actually hold up in court, which never ceases to amaze me.

The world we live in has become one of blame shifting and excuses. Everything that an individual does can be attributed to something that happened, good or bad, in their past. This perpetuates the idea that our entire existence is dictated by a set of experiences over which we have no control, yet are bound to affect us for our entire lives. I, for one, hate this notion with a passion. It means that my actions are not really by choice, but pre-determined by events which have already passed and which I can't change. I don't want everything I do to be so meaningless and trivial. I am more than my childhood experiences. I've made some huge mistakes in my time, and I wouldn't pay to have had the option of sidestepping them. My mistakes make me who I am just as much as my triumphs.

    It saddens me to think that there are people who will never have the joy of learning an important lesson from a huge screw-up. By not learning to take responsibility for both good and bad actions, a person cuts himself off from a massive part of the experience of living. Life requires integrating all of your experiences into one contiguous whole, and then acting, becoming and changing yourself as you move forward; not relinquishing control of your life to a set of foggy past actions. While you may "understand" these actions, you have to make a conscious, active effort to point yourself in the right direction in spite of everything. It is not enough to just "understand;" you must truly take responsibility and embrace self-actualization.

    In any case, it should be clear how negatively this trend affects the quality of life in American society. Responsibility is what directly connects us to our actions, and one who lacks that ability completely is known as a sociopath. I'm sure most everyone reading this is familiar with what sociopaths are like. We've all encountered one at some point in our lives. They lack the ability to see the effect they have on other people. In so many words, they have an extreme inability to take responsibility.

This inability could even be described as pathological. Examining these tendencies can give some insight into how detaching oneself from blame is damaging to everyone. A sociopath is simply the logical outcome of acceptance of responsibility status quo. All sociopaths are unpleasant people to be around. They don't care what they say or do because they can't connect their actions to how it might influence the people around them. At best, they are nasty, rude people; at worst, they are violent criminals.

If you got *really* mad at someone, and you had no notion at all about the consequences of your actions, you might just kill him right? Of course, for a normal person, this would be a fleeting impulse that is easily suppressed- just a random thought. For a sociopath, however, there's no reason not to kill. Why bother restraining oneself when there's no recourse for one's actions?

This is a very extreme case, but I find this attitude popping up alarmingly often among my peers. They demonstrate a refusal to identify how their actions affect others, and a refusal to take responsibility for those actions. One of my friends refuses to pay for the movies. He claims that it's okay because the prices are so high. He even tries to blame the theater for his activities, stating that if only the prices were more reasonable he'd never sneak in. This is just plain ridiculous. To what end should this be taken? Suppose the

Philosophy Junk Food

theater lowers its prices from 8 dollars to 5? Would he all of a sudden decide that 5 dollars is too much and continue sneaking in, stating that, once again, it's the theater's fault? As wrong as it is to sneak into the theater to begin with, why not just admit that he's too damn cheap to pay for the movie, so he's going to cheat the owner out of money by sneaking in. He can at least be authentic about his actions. Delinquent activities and detachment from responsibility seem to go hand in hand.

I have something now that I'd like to share with you. It's another little piece I wrote a while ago about dependability. It's not exactly the same topic as we're discussing now, but it ties in fairly well, and I thought it would be a good corollary to this discourse on responsibility. I must warn you that when I wrote it, I was a little drunk and very angry at the world. I forget exactly what had happened to induce it, but I know it wasn't good. Anyway, for your reading pleasure, an older essay of mine called:

******

A Note on Dependability

The "Me" Generation. Defined, by me, to be a blanket term under which all people in our great nation fall (with the merciful exception of my grandparents' generation- the one that endured WWII). We are a people of boundless selfishness. We know only our own fickle urges and seek only the means to satiate the desire of the moment. One hardly needs to have preternatural insight into our

Responsibility

society to see the symptoms of such a cancer. Let me cite just one multi-faceted example of such a symptom:

We sit at home in front of our modern day messiah, the television. We watch "Judge (insert name here)" the latest real-life courtroom television show. Two people sit squabbling over the future of their child born out of wedlock. It is the woman's third child by three different men. She has no job and lives off of welfare checks. The man already has 7 bastard children and pays just enough child-support to feed each one. Let's see what we can dig up from this grassroots example of American culture.

1) Both parties were too selfish to use protection in the first place because, "It doesn't feel as good."

2) From the woman's side: More children mean bigger welfare checks! Perhaps by the time she's mothered a baseball squad, she'll have enough welfare money to retire. Why bother getting a job when you can just have unprotected sex and bring more future criminals into the world. (Therapists would go out of business if people like her stopped giving birth to their patients).

3) From the man's side: Seven children scattered over much of the US! Commendable job, you have a true talent for impregnating down-on-their-luck women. It's a good thing they have enough to eat from your child-support checks, guess your life is just too busy and important to actually be a father though. Wouldn't wanna cut into your leisure time with dull responsibilities now would we?

Philosophy Junk Food

The outcome of this typical daytime media shock icon is irrelevant. It is a farce. People watch this sort of thing for a good laugh. "All I have to do is watch this and I feel so much better about myself. At least I'm not them!" Ahem. This scene should practically bring anyone to tears. The society in which we live is very ill indeed, and by watching this sort of tripe, people validate it. What kind of people have we become? I see a very disturbing parallel between the decadence of the Roman Empire and the Empire of America. We sit in our sheltered little world, and we expect our every desire to be served up to us on a silver platter. Life is so damned easy for us that we have to throw a fit and complain to Daddy government when things don't go our way. "There oughta be a LAW

1) that I get more money when I have my unprotected pleasure trysts, because THEY OWE ME!

2) that the big conglomerate I work for be held responsible for my stupidity by paying me big court settlements! After all, THEY HAVE A LOT OF MONEY AND I ONLY HAVE A LITTLE!

3) that the government should pay for my retirement because I was TOO SHORTSIGHTED to save for it when I had the chance!

4) that the government PROTECT my children by censoring offensive material because I'm just TOO BUSY to monitor what they watch or listen to!

Etc. etc. etc. It's as if the whole country is stuck in this constant state of self-righteous entitlement like a roving pack of tax-paying two-year-olds.

This disturbing pattern of selfishness has cost us dearly in the area of our "ities:" responsibility, dependability, generosity and reliability. It amazes me how revolutionary people thought the ideas were in the movie "Pay it Forward." "Whoa dude, you, like, get help from people and then in return you help other people. Gnarly." Ahem again. NO SHIT! What do you think the rule was seventy years ago? When someone was stranded out on the road, you helped them for God's sake! When someone needed a place to stay, you offered your guest room! You thought of the consequences of your actions! You could depend on people to help you and they could depend on you! ANYTIME! ANYWHERE! Nowadays, even an altruistic act is selfishly based on convenience. I *would* help you on the side of the road if I wasn't in such a hurry to get somewhere for myself. I *would* let you stay here, but I think it would be easier for me to just call you cab and send you to a hotel so I don't have to bother with you anymore. And, alluding back to the earlier example, I *would* have used protection, but bareback just feels so much better.

If we truly want to send our children into a better world, we need to take a long hard look at how we live our own lives. We need to start considering what kind of consequences our actions have on others. We need to become dependable people again that don't just think within our own limited existential bubbles. The tumultuous path that we walk now can only lead to degeneracy and ruin of our society.

******

Philosophy Junk Food

What a difference a few years make. The angry, white-boy angst was so much more poignant back '01. Oh well, I guess you could say I've "mellowed in my old age" (or something like that). As painful as that was, I do think it has some good, if not venomous, points to make about modern day America. It is very true that we worship the television as we would a holy icon. This has had almost wholly negative effects on our lives. The television should be for entertainment and reliable dissemination of information, that's all. The minute the boob tube started trying to influence our views; we all became the biggest suckers in the world. As soon as someone appears on that screen, we automatically assume that person is

    a) knowledgeable in the subject he is discussing;

    b) has our own best interests in mind; and

    c) is more important than us.

This combination gets us primed to eat whatever they're feeding us. Furthermore, because a, b and c are almost always false, what they're feeding us turns out to be poisoned.

Back in the 40's, some very astute people deduced that television and the mass media in general could potentially be worth a lot of money. It didn't take long for the first television executives to start devising ways of making television work for capitalism. This is not necessarily a bad thing. It is bad, however, when we began to let those same executives pull the wool over our eyes and sacrifice our independent thought for the sake of their profit. The price is waaaaaaaaay too high. Don't blame the executives however; they're just trying to make money. Blame yourself. In order for TV to take over your life you have to *let it happen*. Again we're back to responsibility. You must take responsibility for your own TV viewing habits and, by doing so; the TV is no longer a destroyer.

At first, TV was such a novelty that they could show pretty much anything and we'd be mesmerized. Execs devised shows that demonstrated a good ole' slice of American life. People saw other people doing things that were an idealized vision of typical family activities, only in their living rooms on a personal movie theater. It was like magic. Like anything, however, we got bored with "Leave it to Beaver" and other portraits of "normal" people. We needed more. Executives realized this and started upping the ante little by little. This trend eventually grew into shock media. It works under the assumption that even though people might be disgusted by what they're seeing, it'll keep 'em hooked. It's kind of like a train wreck; you may be retching at the gore, but you can't take your eyes off of it. It worked like a charm. Why else would people watch other people eat bulls' testicles on "Fear Factor," or watch relationships fall apart from lust on "Fantasy Island?" The shock trend didn't just create the reality show phenomenon, it also created new sitcoms based on dysfunctional families, shows devoted to extolling the virtues of sexual promiscuity and still other shows devoted to other people's humiliation; even cartoons were not safe from the "shockwave." If you're a 21st century American, I'm sure you can think of at least three examples of each type of show.

Philosophy Junk Food

The fact that these shows are on the air does not make them bad; the negative effect lies in our reaction to them. The characters in these shows are supposed to be caricatures of normal people. They have one aspect of a healthy personality embellished ad ridiculum and then are put in situations that emphasize that imbalance; it's a theatrical technique. Unfortunately, we've been worshipping that TV since it first arrived in our living rooms fifty years ago, and we take what those talking heads say as gospel. We begin to think that acting in socially unacceptable ways is cool or funny. And it's even funnier if we pass off our mistakes as someone else's fault. We think then everyone's going to laugh, give us a pat on the back and then the credits will roll.

We grow up thinking like this. Many of my peers were raised more by TV than by their parents. It gets etched on our minds that nothing is our fault. We only need to take responsibility when we do something good, and if we mess up, it's a lot cooler and funnier if we blame it on something else. In small doses, this can be a somewhat amusing trait in children. The problem occurs when these children grow up and still think and act this way.

They continue on in a fog, never looking ahead or behind, just acting on whims from day to day. The consequences of their actions no longer matter as they have been completely divorced from any causes. Things just happen. Sometimes the outcome is good, sometimes it's not, but due to their ingrained and profound inability to take responsibility, they truly believe that their personal actions had nothing to do with any results. They shrug, take a drag on the cigarette that will surely kill them one day and repeat the mantra of helplessness and hopelessness they've heard from birth: "Shit happens."

    I feel this is quite possibly the most dangerous trend in our society today. As I said, responsibility is associated with age, wisdom and maturity. It seems as if our nation's adults simply become older without getting any wiser or more mature. We think that as long as we didn't inhale, it's ok. Perhaps a differing belief of the definition of "sexual relations" is the real problem? Maybe we can treat our armed forces like a rich kid's Christmas present? Maybe we all need is to just stand up, take a deep breath, and own up to all those mistakes we made but never admitted to. There, doesn't that feel better?

Philosophy Junk Food

Sex

Speaking of feeling better, wouldn't we all feel better if we got laid tonight? Who cares with whom! That's why God invented bars right? All you need is another warm, willing body and there you go; a prepackaged night of fun! It's not like you have anything better to do. Reaffirm your existence through one-night stands! (That really should have been the title of this book, lots more people would read it)

Over the course of my life, I can think of literally nothing which preoccupies people more, myself included, than sex. It's everywhere; billboards, TV, movies, books, in school, at work, in your mind and at home in the bedroom. The sexual revolution broke down sexual barriers in a big way and now sex is so UNtaboo that it's become a ubiquitous part of any post-Saturday night conversation. "Say dude, that chick you were talking to last night was kinda cute. You bang her?" "Yeah. She was a seriously dumb bitch, but I was really horny." Normally listening to this conversation, I would bite my tongue. Anything that could possibly come out would be severely judgmental. However, this is my damn book and I can say anything I please! So let me start a new paragraph and begin the tirade.

A while ago, I watched the movie "Body Shots" with my friends. It's basically a story about a group of single 20-somethings, half men and half women, and how they live a mundane 9-5 existence, but the weekends are the one time they can cut loose and party. The two groups start separately and eventually meet each other at some club. Being half women and half men, and this being the 21st century, they inevitably all get it on (make the beast with two backs, boff their brains out, play hide the salami, bump uglies, hump, bang, screw, fuck... gee that was fun). I didn't really get this movie.

I think it was trying to be some kind of profound snapshot of modern dating and its implications. It had these aside statements from the characters interspersed throughout the movie where they'd comment on the deeper psychological significance of, say, being tied to the bed and getting a rimjob. These aside statements were supposed to make the viewer really *think* about male-female interpersonal relationships. Well, they definitely made me think how stupid the movie was, that's for sure.

Personally, I found nothing profound about this movie whatsoever. There was no dating at all in this movie; not unless you consider dating to be the act of putting out for someone you've known for approximately an hour. The people are whiny, unintelligent, boring and unpleasant portraits of the most unprofound kind of people I can think of. This is why I was surprised to no end when one of these children of the 90's actually made a somewhat profound statement in one of the dim-witted asides (I'm even gonna put it in bold type because it's so important).

Sex without love is violence.

Let's all take a second to let this mull over in our minds. I simply adore this statement. It speaks to me on two different levels, the contexts of both physical and emotional violence. I have a few

Philosophy Junk Food

things I'd like to say about each of them; I'll start with physical violence.

I know the instant you read **the profound statement** your mind went to Leo Tolstoy and his religion of passivity. What? It didn't? Well for those of you whose minds did go there, you can skip this part. For those of you whose minds didn't, here's the explanation. When he started getting older, Leo Tolstoy (the famous Russian author of War and Peace) decided to create a religion based totally on a doctrine of passivity and non-violence. Under his ideals, it's morally wrong to ever commit any physical violence toward anyone under any circumstances, even self-defense. The tricky part of this doctrine is that sexual intercourse is grouped under the heading "violence." Much to the dismay of his wife, Tolstoy decided that sex, even for the purpose of procreation, was violent and morally wrong. From that point in his life on, he became a quasi-Buddhist celibate dedicated to introspection and enlightenment.

This type of life-style has proven very unpopular with the demographic of 12-90 year old men and women. However, this extreme case can teach us something about the nature of sex as I see it. The act of sexual intercourse is, by nature, an act of domination and violence. Consider the action: The man mounts a woman in a prone position of complete vulnerability and proceeds to pound a hard, unforgiving organ inside a very tender area. This is not disgusting or degrading to either party; it is simply the way things are and have always been. People have been doing it a long time. In fact, in my experience, this perceived loss of control by the woman gained by the man dominating her in such a fashion is what turns both parties on the most; i.e. things were meant to be this way. However, it is not an operation I would undertake with just anyone, especially if I were the penetratee rather than the penetrator.

Would you let just anyone probe around in your mouth looking for cavities? Shucks no! You'd make sure they had a paper on the wall saying that they went to school and are fully qualified to use any nasty dental implements that might come up. That's how I see love, it's like the diploma from the relationship school giving partners the qualifications needed to sleep with one another. I think someone without a DDS would probably commit some serious violence to some hapless soul's mouth. Although this type of violence may not be directly applicable to sex (one hardly needs a doctoral degree to get it on with someone), used as a metaphor it ties nicely into the second kind of violence, emotional.

When you take someone who lacks the necessary sexual credentials into your bedroom, you open yourself up to the limitless possibilities of emotional bankruptcy. "Sex is possible with no emotional attachment. It can just be a fun physical interaction as long as all parties agree that it's just for fun." This is what the media, our peers, movies, books and we have been telling ourselves for quite a while. Casual sex is now the *thing* to do in your late teens and twenties. It's become so ubiquitous that it's reached the level of a rite of passage. I've heard it all: "College is the time to experience new things and meet tons of people. You'll never lack responsibilities like this ever again." "You should really sow some wild oats before you even think about settling down." "This is time in my life I was counting on being with tons of people." and my personal favorite… "You're so lucky you're still so young. You don't have to worry about serious relationships. All the quality time you spend with your girlfriend can be horizontal, and then you can spend all your vertical time with your friends."

Like Communism, this all works wonderfully well in theory. Also like Communism, in application, it fails horribly. I don't care who you are, what gender you are, or where you are in life; you can't have casual sex with no emotional consequences. It just can't be done. I'm positive there are a number of you out there thinking, "Bullshit, I do it all the time!" You are, of course, correct. There is one loophole to this postulate. There is a select group of people that can detach themselves from feelings of intimacy. Call it an emergency shut-down switch; Christopher Lasch calls it the "flight from feeling." The upside to this emergency shut-down is that one can sleep with as many people as he/she wants, whenever he/she wants without falling into that emotional connection trap. The downside is an inability to form a relationship based on anything more than being joined at the pelvis.

I can't tell you how many times I've seen it in my peers. It's uncanny! People that are totally cut off from their own emotions, trying to somehow reconnect themselves by relating to the opposite sex the only way they know how, by sleeping with more and more and more people. It's an endless cycle. Another not so great movie, "40 Days and 40 Nights" depicts this phenomenon quite well. The story goes that a highly promiscuous college student gets a wild hare and decides to give up all sexual gratification for lent. He then proceeds to meet a girl and gets to know her in a non-sexual way. He of course falls in love and a sappy story ensues blah blah blah. The movie treats this as if it were the most profound thing in the world. It's perfectly natural to a college aged male to screw every vagina in sight without a second thought, but the instant he begins to see that there is a person surrounding the vagina, he has a new lease on life and learns to love. Well, for lack of a better term, DUH. No one has ever found love from sex alone. You can find lust that will drive you to spend time with that person and then possibly get to know him/her better and eventually fall in love, but no one has ever found anything deep or lasting strictly from the horizontal rumba. As simple of a concept as this seems to be, it never ceases to amaze me how many people just don't seem to grasp it.

So after this rambling discourse on the psychological effect of sex on a person, we can say two things:

1) No one is capable of sex without some emotional connection save those that fall under #2.

2) The people that are capable of such emotionless sex are cut off from their emotions in an extremely unhealthy way and have difficulty having any sort of real intimacy.

It makes sense that some emotions can't be avoided, and as a corollary, why being disconnected from those emotions is so unhealthy. Let me qualify my next point with a little background information. My former brother in law has a degree in Anthropology and he tantalized me with a little intellectual tidbit about human culture. There are four societal conventions that span across the entire spectrum of human existence. Every single culture no matter how advanced or primitive, no matter how rich or how poor has these conventions. Number one, some sort of recognition of coming of age, i.e. passing from childhood to adulthood; number two, a birth ceremony; number three, some sort of ceremony regarding the death of a clan member and number four, MARRIAGE. There are some cultures that allow one person to have multiple spouses, but no matter what, there is a convention that binds a person to their mate. This makes sense.

From an evolutionary biology standpoint, the rearing of children is the absolute most important thing that any of us will ever do. Ensuring the continuation of the species and of our own genes is our job in life. Now I've heard the argument for the "men as bulls" theory that men have a need to impregnate as many people as possible so many times I'm ill. The theory says that a bull will never mate with the same cow twice; they'll just move along and continue screwing new cows until they eventually die. Apparently, many evolutionary biologists have, in the course of obtaining a Ph.D, missed the fact that humans and cows are different.

On the most basic level, yes, men do have the urge to mate with several different women. However, the two situations are hardly comparable. A calf is born much more developed than a human baby. It's ready to walk within days or even hours of its birth. A mother cow can easily care for it herself until it matures. A human baby is a completely different story. Because our heads are so big to account for our oversized cerebrum, we must be born before we're even close to being finished. The birth canal simply isn't big enough to accommodate a baby that's any more developed. Because we're so helpless when we're born, it's very difficult for the mother alone to care for us. It's possible, but it's much better for all parties involved for mommy *and* daddy to be around and share the work.

Our brains, clever as they are, developed love for this very purpose. Anyone that's been in its vice-like grip will agree that love is absolutely the most overpowering emotion. Hate, envy, anger and joy all pale in comparison. When it comes down to it, we're all controlled by our emotions a lot more than most of us would like to admit, and what better way to overcome our natural tendencies to reproduce with tons of partners than with such a strong emotion. The propagation of our species is too damn important to get screwed up, and since baby has an easier time maturing if mommy and daddy stay together and help one another, love is the perfect solution. Baby will have a greater chance of growing up healthy enough to reproduce and make grandbabies if <u>both</u> parents are around. This is in everyone's best interests since the genes are optimally propagated. Reproducing like rabbits with many different partners is no good if most/all of your offspring will die from neglect.

Being the complex little creatures we are (not to sound corny) built like an onion with two layers. We have an underlying desire to mate with as many people as possible, but with an almost overpowering desire to bond with our mate superimposed on top. We reconcile this by choosing one mate to satisfy both needs, one that can provide children and one that we can bond with. The notion of emotionless sex is a foul bastardization of this natural way. The idea of sleeping with tons of partners feels natural, and at one level it is, but it comes at the cost of stripping away the quality makes us unique from alley cats; namely, our desire to bond emotionally with our sexual partner. Alley cats certainly don't bond with their mates but we do; and we're supposed to in order to improve the lives of our offspring so they can, in turn, improve the life of theirs.

So far, I've defined love in two different ways: one as a qualification for sex and one as a result of sex. This seems contradictory right? Allow me to explain (I won't go into huge detail, a topic as large as love deserves its own chapter, which it gets!). The sex diploma is the beginning of that bond one feels for a partner. It is an exciting combination of lust (physical attraction), affection for the person (personality attraction) and pure nervousness. This feeling is intensified by the act of sex. Along with the intensification, a new emotional bond begins to appear. The emotional bond is the one that lasts; the "important" one. It comes from the understanding and trust that come along with allowing someone to get that intimate with you. Remember my horrifying description of sex as an act of physical violence? What's happened is that you've trusted someone enough to commit that act with them. It's a bonding experience all the way around. The emotional love can grow in leaps and bounds without sex, but the seeds are planted with that kind of physical intimacy. The excitement kind of love is fleeting, but it does serve the purpose of breaking the ice and opening the door for the greater kind of love; the love of emotional bonding.

At any rate, what I've said in the preceding pages can be summed up rather easily. I personally believe that promiscuity is a self-destructive and unhealthy activity. Sleeping with tons of people and suppressing your emotions toward those people can only lead to emotional turmoil and unhappiness in the future. I enjoy sex as much as the next guy, but why would I share something that special with someone I a) barely know, b) might not even like or c) have no intentions of having any interaction other than hip to hip? People of my generation would do well to look at their sexual pasts and see how many of their sexual partners they actually gave a damn about; it might do wonders for their own well-being.

Philosophy Junk Food

Drugs

Speaking of "well-being", since we're not getting laid tonight, we might as well get high. I tell ya, nothing could be finer than parking my ass on the couch and sparking up a fat doobie/snorting a few lines/shooting up a little/getting completely hammered and watching Spongebob Squarepants. Where's the fun in being sober anyway?

Drugs, drugs, drugs. Never have I seen such a simple issue get so overly complicated. Everywhere we look we're flooded by drugs either being glamorized by movies, television and junkie friends or we're flooded by the vilification of drugs from diversion/education programs, other movies, other TV shows or other friends. Drugs have become almost as ubiquitous as sex and it's pretty darn confusing if you ask me. I think motives for using drugs are much simpler than any of these sources make them out to be.

How many of you have heard that there are two ways to use drugs, one as experimentation/recreation and the other as an addict. Let's see a show of hands. One, two, three…. OK that's a lot of you. I could not disagree with this statement more. True, the experimenter hasn't yet crossed over into addiction, and that may never happen, but both the addict and the weekend pot smoker use drugs for the same basic motives.

Let's start with the basic question, why does someone start using drugs? Without a lot of pedantic pontificating, let me get right down to it. People do drugs for flat out escapism/self-destruction.

This applies specifically to my generation. We are assailed all our lives about the dangers of doing drugs. We have D.A.R.E. in elementary school and middle school. Then we have diversion seminars in high school, on top of this we have authority figures of all shapes and sizes peddling ultimatums about what will happen to us if we ever even smell pot, think about alcohol or look at a syringe the wrong way. Because of this, there is absolutely no excuse for anyone that was born after 1975 to not know that drug abuse is bad for you. The act of trying drugs the first time is a knowingly self-destructive act. This act is usually fueled by a combination of rebellion, curiosity and the promise of being just an experiment; a rebellious walk on the wild side. This whole drug thing must be pretty special since so many people have been making such a big deal about it for so long. What harm could it do, it's just an experiment, it's not like I'm an addict, right? Regardless, it still is a self-destructive act, experimental or not.

In spite of knowing what true physical effect it will have, our neophyte user takes the plunge. The road then forks for this hapless and inexperienced drug user. He can choose to believe that he enjoyed the experience, or he can choose to believe he disliked it. It truly is a choice; the bittersweet aftermath of this deflowering is perilous. The knowledge that the act itself is harmful versus the exciting rebellion and truly inexplicable subjective psychological effects makes the decision difficult. There are plenty of people that decide the risk isn't worth it and never touch the stuff against it; a true experiment. If, on the other hand, the person chooses to use again, it no longer falls under the experiment subject head. This is where the story gets to be sad, fair warning. It masquerades as simple recreation, but repeat use like this is much more serious than that.

The rebellion and bizarre nature of the experiences become ever more alluring the more he uses. It soon begins to supplant other recreational activities and becomes the only reward after a hard week. Soon it's no longer an occasional once-a-week thing because, quite frankly, being high is more fun and interesting than normal life. Once he reaches the point of preferring intoxication to sobriety, he has crossed an invisible line. Crossing that line is easy, going back is certainly not.

At this point, the game has become one of escapism and self-loathing. The world is so repugnant that it must be altered to be bearable. The reasons for the repugnance are different for different people. For some, they feel that they are the sole piece of sanity in one seriously messed up world. Others hate themselves for being different, for not being able to "live up to the expectations" of how they perceive the world wants them to be.

The common thread here is a desire to escape. Everyone wants to escape the world sometimes, perhaps even often. What is more fun for a party or even for an afternoon with nothing to do than escaping reality? Remember I said that "recreational use" and "addiction" stem from the same root cause. The effect on the individual and frequency of use are usually what swings the definition one way or the other in the view of society. Either way, it stems from an inability to reconcile uniqueness with status quo assimilation. That's a pretty lonely place to be. But drugs offer a way out. Drugs will never reject you, they'll always be there for you when you need them, they'll comfort you and numb you; they'll make you feel *special*. By nature, drugs are simply a way of giving in to pain and giving up on oneself. It's waving a white flag to an indifferent world.

The problem with this is, if the world is truly indifferent, what is anyone proving? If it *is* the case that the world doesn't care either way if we're happy or sad, you might as well be happy. Intentionally causing harm to oneself isn't going to illicit a pity reaction from the universe at large. We have become such a society of pampered pets that we feel like the universe should care. We, after all, are the center of our own universe, so why aren't we the center of everyone else's?

I never understood the need for after-school programs in inner cities until I understood this underlying motivation. If kids have something worthwhile to devote themselves to, then drugs aren't needed. Basketball won't reject anyone either. It will be there for support just as the drugs are; it'll give something worthy of devotion as well. From here we can very easily make some rather profound assumptions about the nature of love and devotion, and what impact they both have in someone's life, but I'll save that for the love chapter. The meat of the matter is: people have to have something to believe in and, for some people, drugs provide that. They don't require any work or effort, they feel good and they'll always be there for you. A movement away from drugs has to come from the inside,

Philosophy Junk Food

no amount of rehab or external fixes will work if the internals still crave the drug. Now I'd like to talk a little about the war on drugs.

Before I begin let me just say that the following may make me sound like the most hypocritical person in the world. However, I have excellent reasons for everything I say (in my own mind) and this is my book so if you don't like it, I've already got your money! HA!

That being said, I would like to say that the war on drugs is the absolute stupidest government decision since Vietnam. As I said above, I do have reasons for this view (I'm not that irrational!). Let me give an example: Everyone's had at least one lemon car in their life. Man, are those things the pits. You just keep throwing money into them and throwing money into them and throwing money into them and they never work! Finally, after you've had the transmission replaced for the third time you decide to junk the damn thing as a sunk cost and just get a new car. This is the course of action most logical people would take. Who would bother wasting money trying to fix something that's obviously not going to ever work? The US Government, that's who.

Let's come to terms with reality here. The war on drugs is lost. We have failed. No matter how hard we try, we just can't stop the dope peddlers from getting into the country and selling it. We've cracked down on every border, we've instituted drug education plans in schools, we've created rehab clinics aplenty to get addicts cleaned up *and none of it has worked*. None. So why, I implore the audience, do we keep blowing tax money on such apparently useless actions? It has obviously failed us, and we need to abandon the war on drugs immediately.

In lieu of what, you may ask. How are we supposed to stop the peddlers without the war on drugs? How do we stop the meth-labs and crack dens? WHAT ABOUT THE CHILDREN?!?! Well, this is where you begin to think I'm a hypocrite. I personally believe we should legalize all drugs. That's right; I think we should remove all restrictions on controlled substances. "WHAT? Is this the same guy who for pages has been screaming from his soap-box about the evils of drug use? The same guy that says drugs are the ultimate escapist act that is wholly self-destructive in nature???" To save the trouble of coming up with an excuse, I'll admit that yes, I am that guy. Hear me out, however.

Drugs are dangerous, that is a given. There's no doubt about the risk involved in sharing a needle with someone you don't know; about smoking weed at a concert that could have lord knows what else laced in it; about dropping brown acid then becoming convinced that you're a bird ready to fly from the 40th floor. However it's time to face the fact that we're never going to be able to force people to stop taking drugs. Quitting has to be an internally motivated action. The state can't tell people how to live their personal lives, it can make laws, but people don't have to follow them. This kind of legislation only confirms the government's lack of faith in the decision-making capabilities of its people. You might say, "Well what about murder? You're advocating that if enough people start murdering and disobeying the law, the government should just legalize it!" The principle difference here is that drug use only affects the person using it. The government needs to respect peoples' individual choice about what to do to their bodies. Fast food could be said to be just as harmful as many drugs, statistically. But you don't see the government running to outlaw McDonald's. It's because fast food is universally accepted as a choice to the consumer. A person obese from eating tons of McDonald's has only himself to blame. It's time for the government to treat a heroin addict the same way.

In my view, half the problem is the amount of attention government run anti-drug programs attract to drug culture in the first place. The target audience (elementary and middle school students) is intrinsically curious. Just talking about all the bad things drugs can do is going to get their sharp little minds going. They'll begin to wonder what drugs are really like and if they can truly trust what the scary police officer visiting their class is telling them.

However, if the government were regulating the production and distribution of drugs, many risk factors currently in the drug culture would disappear. Drug dealers would disappear; the streets would be safer and property wouldn't get stolen as much since the drugs could get sold at a fraction of the street cost and still turn a profit. Drugs could also be taxed and then used for government projects. Aids to help quit using would be much more readily available and have much less of a stigma attached ("Still using Heroin Bob?" "Nope, I'm on the Methadone patch, Bill."). People could stop worrying as much about the spread of disease through sharing of paraphernalia. The drugs themselves would be pure, so the risks of using "bad X/heroin, tainted weed etc." would disappear. In my estimation, the war on drugs causes more crime than it prevents simply because a seedy criminal element is attracted by the opportunity to turn a quick profit from selling illegal goods (go read an unbiased article about the consequences of Prohibition if you don't believe me).

The thought of our government supporting and taxing the use of addictive and life-threatening substances may make some stomachs turn. Remember tobacco and alcohol though? How is it any different? I smell a double-standard based on some sort of political fraternizing. No matter.

Basically it comes down to this, people have to rehabilitate themselves. Those that government throws money at to try and "help" are not getting any favors. The only true fix is the self-motivated one. It's true that drugs can be a great escape from reality, in fact, that's *all* they are, but they are in essence a self-destructive act. Everyone, myself included, likes getting fucked up in one way or another from time to time, but I don't try to make drugs something they're not. They don't expand my consciousness, they don't generally improve my life and they don't substitute for genuine, sober feelings. They are not love (see Chapter 5 for more), they will not make anyone happy in the long run and they only fit into your job description if you're a rock star.

Rock and Roll

So I was at this Incubus concert a few years ago, and this one dude who was crowd surfing got dropped and totally messed up his leg! They, like, had to stop the show for a while so they could get the guy to an ambulance! It was the weirdest thing ever! The show was the dopest though!!!

Alright, alright, enough unfunny humor. It's really hard to tell jokes, especially ones that require odd intonation, in writing. Anyway, I love rock and metal music. It's just the best as far as I'm concerned; I love lively beats and energetic lyrics. I just love getting pumped up from listening to some goddamn power chords! YEAH!

I need to start me up a band and get signed! Chicks dig guys in bands. Become big and you got girls lining up at your door to get nasty with your hang-low. You know that Gene Simmons has boned over 1000 women? That's just plain crazy. Now, has anyone ever thought about why… (Personal note: I actually was signed on a small label with my band, Skin Flick, back in '02, but the other guys all had to finish "college" and go on to "med school" and "engineering jobs," what a waste)

That is the subject that I would like to examine in this chapter; the "starfucker complex." More precisely, I would like to examine the psychology of celebrity worship; not just rock stars, but all celebrities: models, athletes, movie stars, all that crap. I'm sure that the answer to this question seems patently obvious to many people. People want to get close to celebrities because they're famous.

Rock and Roll

Yeah... but what the hell does that mean? 'Well, they have lots of money.' Yeah... but people must realize that they will most likely be just another notch on the bedpost of a star and won't ever see a dime. 'Well, they're influential.' Yeah... but to someone who has been with dozens or 100's of people in his life, what effect will one more have? 'Well, they're hot!' Yeah... but it's my contention that there are plenty of regular old folks out there that are just as attractive and much, much more approachable.

I'm gonna tell you what I think the real reason is (as if you weren't expecting that). Celebrities have been raised above the populace as a whole and have achieved a perceived property of super-humanity. People are then compelled to become a part of that super human existence even if it means degrading oneself to the point of prostituting one's body. Allow me to elaborate:

The problem lies, once again, in that religious icon with rabbit ears that sits in our living room. I speak, of course, of the ever-present television and the wonderful messages that come out of it. The media shows us a never-ending stream of the "beautiful people" having beautiful times and doing beautiful things. It is a world totally alien to the world of traffic, work and stress that we live in. It doesn't take very long for us to get convinced we are getting screwed here. The famous people get to have all the fun and we get all the shit. They look better in bikinis that we do, they have more money than we do and they get to do all things we only dream about; they basically have the perfect lives. Well let me shatter everything that E! network

Philosophy Junk Food

has taught you. That world is no more real than Middle Earth. It is a fabrication created by networks to keep you glued to the screen so you can absorb all the advertising messages they have lined up for you at the breaks.

Even still, people get wrapped up in this stuff the way they should be wrapped up in their own lives. The paparazzi photography industry is now multi-million dollar. People eat the stuff up. It's sad really; people spend more time agonizing over Brad and Angelina than they do tending to their own problems. Sooner or later, people become convinced that there are the stars, a higher form of existence, and then there's everyone else. Being featured on MTV, E!, on talk shows or wherever else in the public eye constitutes superiority. The object of fascination is no longer among the ranks of "normal" humanity, they are deified.

Once that attitude is ingrained in the mind, people are willing to do whatever it takes to touch that greatness; people want to be closer to their deities. This is the core of the aforementioned "starfucker complex." Why would someone rather have sex with Brad Pitt than with a comparably attractive man in her office? The answer is Brad Pitt's unapproachable "God" status. Fucking Brad Pitt is a quasi-religious experience, whereas fucking Jim from sales is just a boring old roll in the hay with another mere mortal. We get programmed by the media to think that those in the public eye are infinitely more worthy of affection than "regular" people.

To me, this is clearly a case of Nietzschean psychology setting in. For those that aren't familiar with Nietzschean psychology, here's the watered down version. To understand Nietzsche's brilliant critique on the human psyche, we must first look back to the real basic beginnings of humanity. Nietzsche is a cultural relativist. In most basic terms, this means that he believes people's minds are ultimately shaped by the culture in which they were brought up. Our morals, our beliefs and our views on happiness are all a consequence of our cultural experience. Returning to the basic beginnings of humanity, we can see that the number one most important thing to anyone was the clan. Humans were physically unimpressive compared to the predators stalking them. We have poor vision, we're slow, we have no claws and our teeth are a joke. We are like walking french fries to a saber-toothed tiger. Our minds were our one true advantage over hungry, prehistoric beasts. Two heads are better than one right? That must mean three is better than two. And four is better than three… We simply extrapolated this idea of grouping and began living in communities. This "strength in numbers" idea is not limited to humans; most prey animals travel in groups. From the beginning, a person's survival was dependent upon being a member of the group. This is the wellspring of what we now call "society."

To me, this is an indisputable fact. Society is derived from the intrinsic human need to be a member of something larger than itself for its own well-being. The controversial part about Nietzsche's view is that he believes that the "society" is the most damaging thing to a person. He calls the mass of people that make up society the "Herd." This term certainly has a negative connotation, and that is by design. He claims that people in the Herd are mindless drones conforming to a destructive "metanarrative."

The term metanarrative is a technical philosophical term. To the layman, it can be interpreted as any story, code, rulebook etc. that outlines an overarching code of values and applies it to our lives. The root of the word "meta" is "beyond" or "transcending" and "narrative" refers to the story it tells. The most famous such metanarrative is the Bible. The Bible gives us such a framework for our lives. It basically outlines rules of conduct for Western society; our basic rights and wrongs. We want to believe that our actions are fitting into some greater good and that our work is in harmony with the will of the universe. Nietzsche, ever the one for instigating controversy, rejects any and all metanarratives as false. Furthermore, he condemns all that follow any metanarrative (moral codes, religions, etc.) as doddering fools and pathetic members of the Herd. In order to become what we should be, we need to free ourselves from the Herd and abandon all metanarratives.

Needless to say, this is not a popular view. People do not like being called fools or mindless followers, especially when it is their most deeply held beliefs that are to blame. I, for one, am lukewarm about Nietzsche's rejection of all metanarratives. I think they serve an important function in the world and without them, many people would be lost. I do not reject the idea of society and I think it's important to have guidelines through life. That being said, however, I must agree with Nietzsche that the human mind does have a tendency to fall into the Herd. People are attracted very strongly to any metanarrative that makes sense to them. They also tend to be very gullible when it comes to advice given by such a code. This leaves the door open for con-artists and shysters to distort the code and manipulate the followers. Such a manipulation is a force to be reckoned with (look at Scientology for crying out loud). Who better to distort and manipulate our beliefs than the popular media?

Our best friend in this day and age is the television. It provides us entertainment and even companionship. The media controls the content of what we see on television, as well radio, magazines and many things we encounter constantly in our daily lives. The Church of Media is gaining power with each click of the remote. We receive its messages day in and day out. It force-feeds its ideas about society, love, life and happiness alarmingly efficiently. This is the new metanarrative of our society. Much like the Bible drums the Ten Commandments into our heads, the Church of Media drums its beliefs into us. However, where the Ten Commandments were written to better society and to instill moral values into the citizens, the Media's message only masquerades as such. It is a wolf in sheep's clothing. It promises that if you only *buy this product* or *live this lifestyle* then you will be bettering your life and becoming a happier person. Its true motive, of course, is not to help you, but only to separate you from your money.

Philosophy Junk Food

This is all well and good, but how does it apply to the "starfucker complex?" Well, it is through this constant Media barrage that the wonderful fantasy world of the celebrity has emerged. We are the Nietzschean "Herd" being led on by the Media. Through the eyes of E! network we don't see talented actors and musicians showing off their skills for our delight. We instead see the deities of this metanarrative; we the see the apostles and angels and muses of this disconnected fantasy world. And man does it make our drudgery laden lives look like a pile of dog shit. What we see through this diamond camera lens is a never ending party with all the most beautiful people. We see dancing and laughing and flamboyant spending. We see vacations on private jets, days filled with champagne and joy, nights filled with beauty and passion. Not a care in the world, anything and everything at beck-and-call and absolutely NO traffic jams.

To the average person sitting in the living room watching, this is indeed heaven. We have been duped into thinking that what we see through the lens is the new Truth of existence. Like any good religious follower, we yearn to be closer to our gods. We want more than anything to step through that television screen and become one with our deities. This being impossible, we are willing to do anything to touch a part of that radiant world. This inchoate need for closeness expresses itself through the most powerful act we can undertake as humans; sex.

It helps that the majority of celebrities are very attractive people, but that is not the chief mechanism at work here. We think that by having sex with one of these gods among men, we are accepted into that heaven if only for a very short time. We are becoming one with our icon. To most people, regardless of how devout they may be in what ever religion they practice, if you drugged them with sodium pentothal and asked them what their most spiritually significant act has ever been, it would probably be having sex. For some, the line between the divine and the real becomes so blurry that they practically devote their lives to "touching" (fucking) that which they perceive as god-like. From this comes the "groupie"; an interesting euphemism that could just as easily have been "prostitute."

This is a problem. Even people not necessarily interested in having sex with the stars can develop an unhealthy obsession with their lives. The 55" high definition seer residing in our living rooms allow us a running discourse on the comings and goings of our deities. Indeed, I am fascinated to see how people can agonize over celebrities' personal lives while their own friends, mate and children are being alienated. We will allow our own personal lives to go to shambles while are held rapt over how Brad and Angelina are working out.

This is not good for either side. It is this very obsession that can make the life of a celebrity less than comfortable. Imagine someone following you around with a camera when you go to the grocery store, when you fill up your gas, when you are leaving a bar a little tipsy. Everywhere you go, the camera is there, waiting for you to do something stupid or funny so that they can snatch it on film and broadcast it to the world. Imagine always having to agonize over what you're going to wear because, heaven forbid, if you go out wearing something that doesn't match you will be crucified. This is the life of a celebrity being hounded by the paparazzi. Everything they do in public is documented and broadcast to the followers of the Church of Media all over the world. Celebrities are, after all, humans like you and me, but they are expected to keep up the godlike charade or they become a pariah. Behaving as a real person is a betrayal of the faith worthy of being cast into Tabloid Hell, a land where lawsuits are big and libel is rampant.

It is certainly not a good thing to be a devout follower a metanarrative that encourages obsession with distant icons and discourages real relationships with accessible people. On the other side, it is also uncomfortable for those under the microscope to constantly live up to godly standards. This is the origin of the "pressure of fame." What can we do?

Well, the ball is really in the court of the followers of the religion. I believe the facts we need to quell this dependence on the metanarrative are simple and at hand. Here is a brief outline of what I think they are:

1. Celebrities really are people like you and me. This may seem hard to grasp because of so much mental conditioning, but they

are, in fact, just regular people with a talent and an occupation that puts them into prominence.

2. Just because this occupation brings them into your home on your command, you do not have the right to see into their actual lives. What you have a right to be interested in is their work. You have a great appreciation for the work done by the mechanic that fixes your car, but do you want to know where he spent his honeymoon or how he dresses at parties or if he gets drunk as a skunk at said parties and throws up? No. Such information is understood to be his business, not yours.

3. Redirect the time and energy you waste prying into celebrities' private lives toward repairing your own private life. Reconnect with your family, start a new hobby, learn a new language or whatever to improve yourself. Hell you could even take up guitar and try to become a rock star too!

Either way, a reduced emphasis on the idea of fame superiority would make life a lot easier on the performers as well as the viewers. We could go ahead and let celebrities be people. People would stop buying tabloids, paparazzi photographers would go back to robbing convenience stores and the E! network would finally quietly die. Does it get any better? We could simply enjoy the chosen craft of our favorite actors, musicians, athletes etc. and they could go ahead and entertain us without fear of slipping up and falling from heaven.

Philosophy Junk Food

Love

Ah, love; the glorious nectar of life that the luckiest of us will truly taste. Nothing is sweeter. This is the most important thing in any of our lives; period, end of story. Every single major human action can be traced back to the need for love. This is, without a doubt, 100% true and I dare anyone to challenge me on this. Allow me to present my argument to this end.

I allude back to my chapter of drugs. Remember how I asked the question, why do people use drugs? The answer I presented was that drugs are a form of escapism. That is all well and good but I want to take it further. Recall again that I stated, somewhat in passing, that drugs will always be there for a user, them will never reject him. They cling to the drugs as they would a puppy because (in addition to physical addiction) they have come to love the drugs; they know that the drugs will never cheat on them or fail them. Traditional knowledge classifies this as fear of abandonment or fear of rejection. The fact of the matter is, "abandonment" is a terrible word choice for this phenomenon.

Abandonment implies some sort of passivity in the face of some object/person being present and then altogether absent. Nothing has left the subject; there is only a perceived loss or emptiness without an acute cause. A much better word choice is simple loneliness. It seems a pitiful explanation for such an omnipresent social problem, but I don't believe that there is a better explanation. The drugs will, in theory, fill a void left open by a lack of anything more substantial to love. Fear of rejection, abandonment and bitter loneliness are all symptoms of this same void. Some choose drugs to fill it, some don't, but in the end it all comes down to a lack of love for anything concrete. In support of this, I draw on personal experience and a few tidbits from Aristotle.

I have noticed in my life that I have three modes. I can either have a steady girlfriend who I am crazy about, I can be totally into my soccer and playing all the time or I can throw myself into school like a librarian on speed. If none of these occur, I have a fourth option which is pure self-destruction; I crave booze and I don't follow my responsibilities. Anyone of these things provides the same result; I am devoted to them and they allow me the release of seeing my devotions produce utilitarian results. I can love my soccer and it will always give me satisfaction, physical fitness and competitive fulfillment. I can love school to death and I'll see results in my GPA. I can love my girlfriend and she'll give me companionship and love in return. I can love my booze and it will always numb me. Of all these options, of course I would choose having a loving girlfriend over any of the others. It's much more fulfilling to have a breathing cuddle buddy than a pile of books.

The optimum here, of course is to find a balance, a happy medium; but this is much more difficult than it sounds. If one option is providing everything I need, then why fix it if it ain't broke? This happens with plenty of people. I can't tell you how many times I've heard complaining from friends (and out of my own mouth) that a

Philosophy Junk Food

member of the group has gotten hitched up with a steady and, as a result, is never around anymore. This happens to everyone. I can feel it myself when I am in a relationship, I begin to go to school only because I know I *have* to and then all my free time is spent with that special someone. This is not a bad thing; it's just a bad form of insurance. It sure does suck to get out of a relationship and find out that none of your friends like you anymore because you've been AWOL for the past 4 months, or that you now suck at soccer because you haven't played, or that your grades are now in the toilet etc. etc. etc.

Anyway, I digress. Returning to my previous point, I realize in my life that I have basically four concrete goals to pursue in my life. It doesn't matter what it is, but I must have some goal in mind to follow at any given time in my life or I am lost. This is a standard teleological model of human existence. "Telos" comes from the Greek for "goal" and basically states that human action is dictated by a series of goals those actions attempt to achieve.

This ties in wonderfully to where Aristotle fits into this big mess. In all seriousness, how many of you out there have perused Book 1 of Aristotle's <u>Nicomachean Ethics</u>? Well for those lucky few nodding their heads, this'll be a treat! You'll finally get some use out of those philosophy classes you had to take in college (other than trying to get in girls' pants by waxing philosophical about subjects you know absolutely nothing about, sense a little personal history here?). In summary, Book 1's main concern is the ultimate end of human action.

Aristotle begins by stating the obvious fact that any action in someone's life has a goal; or telos as we just discussed. This seems simple enough. Things start to get dicey when we start playing the "why?" game. Anyone remember when you were little and you'd ask why the sky is blue? When answered you'd then ask "why?" again and again as more answers came in. This is what is known as a regression of questions. If examined, we can see that goals regress in such a way as well. In fact, goals are nested. One goal is accomplished solely for the purpose of attaining a proximal goal further up in the hierarchy. The question is where this regression of nested goals and actions ever ends.

I will illustrate this with a regression of questions about actions and goals culminating in the final basic goal of human existence: "Why did you get on the bus?" "To go to the job interview." "Why did you go to the interview?" "To get the job." "Why did you want the job?" "To get money." "Why did you want money?" "To have a good quality of life." "Why did you want a good quality of life?" "To be happy." And there it is! Aristotle makes this simple point that the ultimate goal of any human action is to achieve happiness. In reality, he claims that people want to achieve a state of *eudaimonia*, which is a Greek word basically describing the state of "human flourishing." However, it is normally translated and understood to mean a state of happiness. That's the point that I like to take home. He goes on to discuss *how* he believes everyone can achieve happiness, but I think that has less value. I would like to take it from here and continue along my own line of logic.

Yes it is true that the ultimate goal of every action is to achieve happiness, I'll give Aristotle that much. But my ideas of how to go about this differ greatly. He believes that everyone must perform their specific "ergon," which roughly translated, means "common action" or "function." In this way, a bee's ergon is to pollinate flowers and make honey and a caterpillar's ergon is to become a butterfly and make lots of little babies. I can halfway agree with this; however he believes that humanity's ergon is the pursuit of rational thought. He believes that what sets humans apart and serves as their true function is rationality. I disagree totally. Yes, rationality does set humans apart from, say, a caterpillar. However, I do not believe it is the gateway to happiness. I think it is false logic to assume that just because our rationality makes us unique in some ways; it is the way to have a happy life. Rational thought is definitely a useful tool, but it is far from the gateway to happiness.

Knowing the name of the chapter you're reading will help a lot in guessing exactly what I think the gateway is. Maybe I'm just a hopeless romantic, or maybe it's that I'm 24 years old and haven't gotten old enough to grow cold and cynical, but I really think that the true path to happiness is love and that humanity's ergon is the pursuit of it. It doesn't have to be the love a person, that's far too general. Alluding back to the beginning of this chapter, I claimed that I could be happy being wrapped up in soccer, school, a girl or booze. I will fall in love with any or all of these things and gain life fulfillment out of them. Of course, loving a girl is the most fulfilling both biologically, for obvious reasons, and emotionally because she is capable of returning the love. By returning the love, she is, in turn, fulfilling her ergon as well. I believe that the Aristotelian happiness gained from fulfilling your own ergon is increased exponentially if you help fulfill someone else's ergon at the same time.

In a more practical, less spooky philosophical light, love as ergon makes sense from a biological standpoint as well. Thinking back on the Sex chapter, I stated that love is a type of diploma that gives your partner the right to have sex with you. I also stated that in the eyes of Mother Nature, our absolute prime function is the propagation of our genetic material and the continuation of the species. This is overlaid with societal expectations and advanced thought, but propagation is still our most primal function. I spoke of love as reconciliation between this primal need to mate, and our advanced cognitive evolutionary adaptations, i.e. rational thought.

In Aristotle's eyes, the Hedonists (those who only pursued pleasures of the flesh for happiness and fulfillment) were always searching for a "low" form of happiness and were no better than cattle in a field. This extreme puritanical view is incompatible with reality. The fact of the matter is humans were meant to have sex and to enjoy it. We were also meant to love and be loved. My analogue to the Aristotelian Hedonists would have to be people that only love any

Philosophy Junk Food

kind of physical object (drug addicts, misers relentlessly pursuing money, sluts and man-whores looking only for the next conquest etc.). Happiness can be achieved on some level but it will always be "subordinate to" the happiness gained from loving and receiving love. This would account for my increased contentment with life when in love with a girl rather than my schoolwork. So, I conclude that there are two types of love:

1. Love that is given and not returned
2. Love that is given and returned

With type two being superior to type one and true happiness found only when type two love is found and kept.

WARNING – Terrible Digression Follows Hehehe, I just can't resist an opportunity to switch gears rapidly and suddenly. As I sit here and write this, it's Valentine's Day. I just got back from the grocery store and see that love is in the air. Flower arrangements adorning everything, balloons with the words "Be My Valentine" written neatly across in bubbly pink letters, Champaign bottles springing up like non-sequiturs in the personal hygiene section. It's odd however. This holiday has always seemed enigmatic to me. Coming off a 5 page tome on how love is the overreaching force of happiness in the world, it seems somewhat of a cop out that we have this one lousy day with which to celebrate it. My standing on the whole ordeal is that it is basically a fabrication of greeting card companies (a tired, but accurate, complaint of many dateless wonders). True, I enjoy having an excuse to celebrate, but what's stopping people from getting flowers for their sweethearts any other day? I'm not at all cynical about it; I love going on a fancy date with my girl, and being mushy and romantic but it just seems kind of ridiculous. I compare Valentine's Day to another time honored greeting card company creation, Mother's Day. Let's get real here people, for all the crap most of us put our mothers through; every freakin' day should be Mother's Day. Why in God's name do we need a day set aside to appreciate our moms?

    I picture it this way, the big-wigs at Hallmark are sitting in a darkened room sometime in the 1950's, frantically trying to come up with ideas on how to cash in on the new, post WWII prosperity. "Well," they must've thought, "we have here in Valentine's Day, a holiday that revolves around giving cards to those that you admire. It's been around for hundreds of years, now it's time to exploit it!" Hence, it became what it is today. We once again throw ourselves on the altar of consumerism as the ultimate show of sacrifice and devotion to our partners. It kind of makes me sick how this obsession can creep its way into even the most cherished form of human emotion and expression. This is a chronic symptom of the "low" form of happiness (loving of a physical object) masquerading as the higher form of happiness, love that is given and returned.

    When we are young and first starting to feel that wonderful rush of hormones, we are often warned to not mistake true love for lust. When such feelings are awakening for the first time, it is often difficult to tell when you have real loving feelings toward someone or if you just want a piece of dat ass. Obviously, sexual feelings are a part of love, but there is much more to the real McCoy, whereas, with lust, the sexual feelings are the full extent. This is a textbook case of type one vs. type two love. Lust clearly corresponds to type one love because it is the love of another's body only and that person's body is incapable of returning the emotion of love. When was the last time a nice set of boobs or muscular arms expressed feelings of love toward any of us? This is why lust is an ultimately unfulfilling exercise. It may be a lot of fun, but it is not the pathway to happiness.

Now, returning to my statements about consumerism relating to love, it seems patently obvious that loving someone more or less based on what kind of gifts they give you is preposterous. It is obviously type one love again; the money that the other person possesses being the true object of affection. *Everyone* thinks that they aren't materialistic in that way. *Everyone* will agree with me that you should never base feelings on gifts and other corporeal considerations. However, lack of hypocrisy has never been a strong part of the human condition. Of course gifts, money, fancy dinners, nice cars etc. etc. etc. are going to influence feelings. I'm not saying this is bad thing. If the feelings backing up the actions are sincere, then it can be a wonderful symbol of affection. But that's all it is, just a symbol. (I will expound on symbology and how it fits into my picture of the world a great deal in chapter 7, but you'll just have to wait!) The problem is, we humans are such trusting little creatures, and we can easily be duped as to the idea wrapped up in this symbol. We can think it has loving feelings defining it when in fact it is only a tool being used to get into our pants.

This is not the worst scenario, however. Being fooled by an unscrupulous individual speaks badly not of the receiver but of the gift-giver. At least the receiver's "heart is in the right place," meaning that the receiver is giving love and believes it's being returned. The gift giver is simply lustful and using any means necessary to love the receiver's body and not the receiver.

The worst scenario is one in which the receiver loves only the material objects received. This is a cruel way of deceiving oneself. Eventually the love for the money can become mistaken for love of the person. In each case, constant giving of love while receiving none can damage a person's perspective on what love and, in turn, happiness is. This is one major reason why there is a booming industry for self-help books that explain how to find and keep love. This, in itself, is rather ironic considering that the cause of the problem initially was consumerism, love of money/material objects, whatever you want to call it, so the solution that follows is a construct of that same capitalist mentality. There is an endemic societal problem, and someone wants to cash in on it. Unfortunately, since we are so numbed to the bombardments of consumerist minutia flying out of the TV, radio, billboard etc. that we miss this fact. We begin to think that the self-help book author is the one that really understands us and loves us so why don't we go pay $19.95 for the latest

Philosophy Junk Food

installment of <u>Let Me Fix Your Screwed Up Life</u> by Dr. I-Got-My-PhD-Online.

    The solution to this is simple. Everyone has the ability within themselves to heal and love. The trick is to not let yourself get swayed by the altar box in the living room. Giving love and receiving love is the way to get started on that road. Reach out to those that do love you and let them help you. They surely know a lot more about you than a self-help book. The true path to happiness is through type two love; the type that when you give, it gives back. Even if you don't have anyone in the world to love at the moment, go take up a hobby and love that! It's better than doing drugs or convincing yourself that you're fundamentally flawed and will never get better.

    You will become a better and more interesting person. Once you begin to feel that you deserve love, and you give love the same way you expect to receive it, something will come along that will change your life. I know it's about as cheesy as an after school special, but everyone deserves true happiness, not love of material objects pawned by charlatans. Whatever you do, just don't become cynical and say love is a fraud. That is the most tragic form of resignation I know.

Love

Commitment

My generation is severely commitment-phobic. That single statement sums up the entire content of this chapter so, if you're in a hurry to try and get your money back for this book, you can skip it altogether and save yourself my long explanation.

******

Since you're still reading I take it you actually have some modicum of interest in this book and I will gladly continue. As I was saying, my generation is severely commitment-phobic. We relish the idea of keeping options open as long as humanly possible and vacillate endlessly about seemingly trivial decisions. Few concepts are more horrifying than "missing out" because we were already committed to something else. This is revealed throughout our daily lives. The choice of where to go out to dinner is agonizing because of the fear that we may make a "poor choice" and the enjoyment of our meal will not be maximized. We fear committing to one cell phone plan because the next better one may come along and, once again, we'll miss out. We can't stand the thought of being in a serious relationship because then we will lose the opportunity to knock boots with the next hottie that wanders by.

I have seen staggering amounts of evidence to this end evinced in my peers. The recent winning market strategy for cell phones is a "no strings attached" plan. With this, you are free of the contractual obligation to use the phone for a set period of time. A recent article in a well-known men's interest magazine featured an interview with Daisy Fuentes where she claimed that marriage is just another contract to be avoided. We are the generation of the anti-plan. A plan to go to the movies or bars even a day in advance makes some of my peers squirm. The thought of having any commitment at all, no matter how small seems to be unacceptable. Some of these examples are clearly benign. It is also expected to have a certain degree of youthful freedom from commitments that require sacrifices or compromises. However, I believe that this is a burgeoning social problem that began with the Baby Boomers and is spiraling out of control with subsequent generations.

My grandparents' generation returned from World War II to a changed nation. Clearly the defining event in the United States' ascent to the rank of world superpower, World War II launched our nation into an unparalleled period of prosperity. Upon returning home to this booming economy and heightened national spirit, the logical thing to do was to start making babies at an unprecedented rate. The bulging demographic of our society known as the Baby Boomers entered a world with seemingly endless resources and choices. The post-Great Depression/World War II land of milk and honey was the great reward for my grandparents' generation. They had to suffer through the hard times to earn such prosperity whereas, for the Boomers, this was simply the status quo. They never knew the hardships that had to be overcome to get to this Promised Land. Wealth, prosperity and an endless amount of attractive choices were simply expected. Try as their parents might, they could not educate the Boomers about the need for humility and the virtue of temperance. In a world where everything was available on a silver platter, these ideas were far too abstract to be absorbed.

Why commit yourself to one thing, whatever that may be, when there are boundless, equally attractive other things? I use the ambiguous word "thing" because it could literally be anything; a car, job, spouse, etc. The capitalist system was an absolutely perfect venue. Market diversity shot through the roof. We could now walk down the cereal isle of our local supermarket and choose from dozens of brands. Choices barraged us from every angle and we had no idea if we should be eating Post Toasties or Sugar Smacks. What were we to do?

The old saying that "the grass is always greener on the other side of the fence" illuminates the problem associated with having so many choices. Because there were so many options, a fear of always losing out on the one option that would make you the happiest developed. Swimming in this sea of options, it was universally concluded that it was better to avoid making any decision than risk being unhappy with an irrevocable one already made.

As this inchoate attitude coalesced in the minds of Boomers, the Boomers themselves began growing up and having babies (my generation). These babies were indoctrinated into a similar world of great prosperity and deep fried foods. However, unlike the Boomers, whose parents had gone through real hardship and survived, our parents *were* the Boomers, the inventors of the "options open" culture. This lack of any ambiguity or misalignment of apparent reality with our parents' opinions made commitment a serious boogey-man.

This spells trouble for my generation. We can already see the rather disastrous effect this attitude has already had on society by looking at how badly the Baby Boomers have screwed up. Granted, not all societal problems are the fault of the Boomers and the ones that are their fault are not all created by the commitment-phobia. However, I do believe a good portion do fit this criterion. The most obvious problem and the one that I will focus on, is the degradation of the institution of marriage, and how that degradation has affected the American ideas about family.

Societal opinions about marriage have drastically changed in the last fifty years. What up until relatively recently was considered a joyous and fruitful union for life has become a joke. We now view marriage as some kind of lifelong prison sentence. Our bachelor/ette parties are reminiscent of the last feast before a prisoner is executed. The thought of being "tied down" is akin to having a third arm surgically attached to one's body. It is crystal clear that this attitude cannot be attributed to cold feet. Divorce is quick, painless and pervasive. People engage now in "trial marriages." "Till death do us part" has mutated into "till we get bored," or "till the money gets tight," or "till someone prettier/smarter/richer comes along." This is defended by endless rhetoric about how "marriage is a difficult compromise" or "a lifelong commitment to one person is simply not possible." While this may appear true to some, in reality these are just immaterial excuses. In the 21st century United States, marriage is not forced on anyone. People (for the most part) know what they're getting into, yet they bolt at the first sign of trouble, giving up incredibly easily. Still, people are compelled to marry and look for love and happiness even after one or multiple failed marriages. Why is it all so unsuccessful?

    The answer, as you might expect, is related to my and my parents' generation's inability to commit. I will draw a very illustrative example from the movie "High Fidelity." I consider this movie to be the authoritative critique on modern relationships and love. The main character has just gone through a difficult break-up. Being in his mid-thirties and alone, he has somewhat of an existential love crisis. In an attempt to figure it all out, he goes back and analyzes the circumstances of each of his worst break-ups of all time. After much soul searching, he concludes that his problems are associated with underwear. At first when he starts dating a girl, he just sees the sexy lingerie. As the relationship progresses, however, eventually the lingerie gets replaced by regular cotton panties. No matter what, the lingerie never persists. He then becomes bored, dumps her, and starts looking for the next set of sexy lingerie. What he eventually realizes is that the lingerie is just a fantasy. One snapshot of a person, but not a reality in itself. The fear of eventually seeing the cotton panties keeps him from ever fully entering the relationship. By keeping his options open, he was committing relationship "suicide."

People keep hunting for love and happiness but they keep looking in the wrong place. They keep looking for the lingerie instead of focusing on how happy they could be if they jumped in with both feet and reveled in the commitment. People insist on keeping their options open for so long that before they even realize it, everything has passed them by. This, in my opinion, is a major contributor to all the divorce problems in our country. People flit from one significant other to the next, constantly chasing after something more until one day they wake up and realize that if it continues, they will die alone. As a result, they snap up the first person they find that shows any promise as a mate and marry him/her. However, from years of commitment dodging, they never learned how to actually commit to such a relationship and the marriage is doomed to fail.

As a nation, because of our great prosperity and wealth of choices, our attitudes have become skewed to the point where we are unable to differentiate between our choice of mate, and our choice of cereal. This obsession with newness, with the metaphorical lingerie, has transcended even our most life-changing and important decisions. We may be thrilled to find a new type of cereal that we absolutely adore. We may in turn continue to buy that cereal for a few months, being completely devoted to it. After those months, however, we become kind of bored with it. It's not that we don't like it; we just don't adore the way we used to. Soon after, we try and become infatuated with another type of cereal, thus continuing the cycle. This attitude has now pervaded our consciousness to an almost fundamental level. The idea of having only one cereal choice in the supermarket is almost unfathomable to any American. Thus, it has grown to encompass our entire lives, including possibly the most important choice of our lives, our spouse.

Obviously, with cereal, this is a harmless exercise. When it comes to inanimate and unimportant choices, like cereal, variety is the spice of life. Our problem lies in not knowing where to draw that line. For the reasons I outline in the Love Chapter, love, as well as two parent families, are essential to the continued evolution of humanity. Therefore, this laissez-faire attitude toward commitment and marriage cannot be allowed to continue.

I've been using marriage as an example to illustrate this phenomenon, however there are other areas that are affected; our choice of livelihood, for one. The real problem here is the way in which commitment is viewed. Humans have a tendency to only look at what they don't have, never what they do have. Our consumerist culture of unbridled acquisition illustrates this dramatically. We always need something better or different. This, combined with our unlimited choices, has created the perception that committing to anything; especially a spouse or job is purely an act of desperation when no other more attractive options are available.

Commitment

We have programmed ourselves to attune only to the lingerie, missing how great the cotton panties can be. Not many of my peers appreciate how wonderful it can be to attain that level of comfort with a mate. The closeness that comes from that kind of familiarity far outweighs the thrill of a new affair, if you look at it the right way. In fact, getting too comfortable with a significant other is considered a bad thing to my generation. It's a sign that you should be getting out and looking for fresh meat. This is simply ridiculous. We need to realize that by relentlessly pursuing the newness, the thrill and the lingerie, we are chasing a phantom that can never be fulfilling in the long term. It's almost like a drug addict constantly in search of the next hit. If we can learn to appreciate the cotton panties and the comfort then we can start correctly searching for the right job or the right mate. This will only make us happier in the long run.

Ideas, Symbols and Sources

At the expense of sounding ridiculously academic, I want to ask one question. The answer to this question is of paramount importance, because, should it be unsatisfactory, the whole of this work will be meaningless. That would mean I wasted an awful lot of time and effort for nothing. The question is, of course, what is reality?

I realize that philosophers have fairly bare-knuckle boxed with this question for much longer than the internet has existed. Furthermore, I realize that my assumption to know a goddamn thing on the subject ranks on the audacity scale somewhere around Al Gore's claim to have *invented* the internet. However, as I've said before, this is my work and I can say anything I please. Therefore, I can clearly say, with absolute certainty, that I have solved the problem and discovered the true nature of reality.

Skeptical? I don't blame you. I have read statements such as these many times over and each time I call the author very ugly names and arrogantly think to myself, "What makes this guy think he knows his ass from a hole in the ground? I'm waaaaaaaay smarter than him; I bet I could do a much better job." Well, to all of you thinking this right now, I look forward to your hate mail. Moving right along, I want to lay the ground work.

If you want to put a label on this, you might call it my metaphysics. Admittedly, this term is far too advanced for my ideas. It might be more fitting to call it my australopithephysics because it must go through a few more evolutionary stages to be considered developed enough to fit the former moniker. How then, does one go about describing the whole of reality? To begin, I must first look to primary source information about how reality manifests itself. To do this, I can only rely on my own perception of reality. Since I have no proof that the beings external to me are independent of my own thought process, it would be improper to initially confer with them. So, beginning with my own perception, I can say with a meager amount of certainty that I see objects around me. If I am unable to make such a claim then my whole idea falls apart, so let's assume that I am accurate in perceiving objects. I am also aware of myself as a sentient being. This too is a fairly large logical jump but let's accept it as true for the sake of this argument as well.

Now, continuing my examination of myself and the world around me, I notice a most puzzling consequence of my "sentience;" my ability to think and self-reflect. Personally, this is perhaps the most puzzling and troubling of all metaphysical problems: what are these ideas and thoughts and where do they come from? Here I sit, then, in front of my computer. I perceive the objects around me, I perceive myself and my own sentience and I perceive the ideas flowing from myself. In fact, I can perceive those very ideas as they are translated and typed onto the screen. It is as if I am creating a symbol for those ideas using my learned tools of language. I am giving said ideas a physical manifestation in my reality. Interestingly, I seem to have been given the ability to create something physical (my type-written language) from something certainly unphysical (the ideas behind the type). This is significant.

With this in mind, let's explore the question of how any physical object is created in reality. Still working within the framework of my single reality, my single primary source, I look at other objects in my apartment. The computer, the pencil, the stapler, all created "artificially." At some point in their existence, these objects had to be an idea. Ah ha! Perhaps these objects bear similar properties to my type-written word. I thought my thoughts, and then transcribed them to the screen, thus creating something physical. The stapler on my desk I can confirm is a physical object in my reality, however, I did not think of it or create it. However, we can safely assume that somewhere, somebody came up with the idea for a stapler and created one. This is the first necessary secondary source encountered in this analysis. So, assuming that the stapler was, in fact, created in this manner, this confirms to a certain degree the existence of other sentient beings like me, thinking and creating. The existence of other objects in the apartment seems to bear out this fact. I can now include the secondary sources around me (other people) into the "consensus reality" that we apparently share. The secondary sources, by definition, have the ability to think and create, like me, but independent of my own efforts or consciousness.

Continuing my scan of the apartment I can describe almost everything within using this method of idea manifested to physical object. I run into a problem when I find a pebble I tracked in lodged

Ideas Symbols and Sources

on my doormat. This is certainly a physical object, yet I can think of no one that created it. It is almost certainly older than all human life on Earth. It seems to exist independently of my system. This is a major problem. In fact, I do not know how this object was created at all. In the case of my stapler, I can at least imagine a factory somewhere making these objects, all based on a template that originated from some secondary source's idea. The pebble, however, has me stumped.

The problem with the pebble lies in how to classify it. I wish to know the origin of the pebble itself. I claim that this fact is immaterial. The important thing is that I immediately identified it as a pebble, a familiar object. Somewhere in my mind existed the notion of "pebble." This notion popped to the surface when I looked at the object, much in the same way as when I looked at the stapler. The idea of pebble was assigned to this object at some point in the past which then forced the object into a role in our consensus reality. At that moment, the pebble was created. Previously, it had been an unperceived, unknown thing to our consensus reality. This concept has mild parallels to the question of if a tree falls in the woods and no one's around, does it make a sound? Instead of answering yes or no, I say that it is an irrelevant question to ask. The pebble, prior to its assignment as "pebble" from someone's idea, was just like this sound. It did not exist in any part of our consensus reality and was, therefore, unimportant. So rather than being directly created by a human being, the pebble was created as a symbol of an idea. Using this definition, all of the objects in my apartment can be described. Each object, whether it be a direct creation or an ideological creation is nonetheless a *symbol* of an idea.

It now seems as if there are three distinct "things" in the world: sources, ideas and symbols. How can we tell them apart though? If all things can be regarded as symbols, then what's to stop me from degenerating consensus reality back into individual reality and say that all the secondary sources around me are symbols? For that matter, why not go the whole way and say that ideas are just symbols too, created by myself as an abstraction of what's really happening?

Well, let's begin with the second point. If my ideas are just symbols, then they have to be a symbol of some other idea, which is a symbol of an idea which is a symbol of an idea which is a symbol of an idea… This could go on for a while. I trust I make my point though, that if my ideas are symbols, then that starts an infinite regression where nothing makes sense at all. Being a physicist, I like to avoid infinities and things not making sense. To my satisfaction, this proves that ideas are not symbols. What about the secondary sources though? Are they merely symbols? I claim that they are not because they have the ability to create ideas which manifest as symbols completely independent of my own ability to create ideas. I exert no control whatsoever over other people's ideas, yet they go about creating them. This also proves to my satisfaction that other sources are not symbols.

So basically, my metaphysics consists of three primary objects:

1. Sources – The creators of ideas. The actual mechanism or origin of ideas is quite baffling and beyond my purview as an amateur philosopher
2. Ideas – Abstract objects unique to each Source; used in individual reality to parse the world and create/reidentify symbols
3. Symbols – The physical manifestation of an idea, be it something that a source physically created or assigned an identity to in the consensus reality

I believe that "sentient being" can be synonymous with "source" in this case. One could argue that I gave no specific boundaries or guidelines to define "sentience" rigorously. I believe the distinction between sentience and non-sentience can be found in the distinction between "individual" and "consensus" reality. A sentient being must be able to demonstrate that he/she adheres to consensus reality in the same way we do in each situation. I believe it is very difficult to show this with the family cat.

One thought-provoking counterexample to this definition of sentience would be in the case of schizophrenic person. We would like to believe that this person is, indeed, sentient, however the way in which this person perceives reality is certainly skewed from that of consensus. Should he be considered non-sentient? Does he have some insight into the world beyond the consensus reality? What causes him to have such a drastically different perception of reality from the consensus? The popular opinion is that a chemical imbalance in the brain causes these abnormalities. Empirical evidence seems to bear this out due to the fact that anti-psychotic drugs seem to correct this imbalance and return the patient to consensus reality in most cases. Is this the whole story though? This really addresses the debate over whether all consciousness is seated in the physical (i.e. it's all chemicals) or some hybrid of the physical and the ethereal (i.e. the soul is non-physical and exists). I am not prepared to fully explore how this affects my theory so, for the time being, I'm simply going to exclude mentally ill people from my analysis of reality.

Continuing on, let us return to the question of the origin of the pebble and how it relates to the question I have just posed; is the universe strictly physical or is it a hybrid? I previously stated that the question of the pebble's creation was immaterial. Indeed, I believe this to be true when it comes to the question of our consensus reality and how to process it. However, having come up with a satisfactory practical theory of our everyday reality, I'm ready to start tackling some bigger problems, like the creation of the pebble question.

Well, where did the pebble come from? This question, like many others, will give you a very different answer depending on who you ask and will even change when the same person is asked at different phases of his life. A geologist will tell you that it is a tiny piece of the Earth's crust that has broken off from erosion or human activity. Ask him where the Earth's crust comes from and he will tell you that it formed when the ball of molten magma that was the proto-Earth began cooling and the outermost layer (the crust) cooled first. Ask him where the proto-Earth came from and he will tell you to go talk to an astronomer.

So you find an astronomer and you ask her where the proto-Earth came from. She will tell you that as the solar system was forming, the tiny particles of dust at this distance from the proto-Sun accreted together over millions of years and eventually formed the hot, liquidous mass that was the proto-Earth. Ask her where the solar system came from and she will tell you that a large area of dust and gas began condensing billions of years ago. 99.9% of that gas and dust would go into forming the sun and the rest would go into forming the solar system, much in the same way the proto-Earth was formed. Ask her where the gas and dust came from and she will tell you that it's part of the Milky Way Galaxy and that there are billions of other galaxies that make up the universe and, to our knowledge, most work the same way ours does. Ask her where the universe came from and she will tell you to go talk to a theologian.

You find a theologian and ask him where the universe came from and he will tell you without skipping a beat that it came from G-d. Of course, most everyone reading this did not need a long passage to come to that conclusion. However, I believe that it is helpful to see exactly how the pebble traces back to a fundamental question of where it all came from. Indeed, it would be equally as simple to trace the stapler back to its ultimate origin in the same way. It came from a factory where it was constructed of raw materials which came from the Earth which came from the crust etc. etc. Indeed, it seems easy enough to come up with a *practical* and useable metaphysics when we dismiss the origin of the pebble question, but once we acknowledge that question, it's a whole different ballgame.

In a way, avoiding that question is a way of preserving one's sanity. Avoiding it allowed me to parse up the world into 3 easy categories in just a few pages with few, if any, holes. Taking that question into account opens us up to literally millennia of debate and millions of pages written on the subject. I'm clearly stepping on hallowed ground here with this question. I'll do my best not to flub it up too badly.

To begin, let us presume the existence of "G-d." I put this in quotations for the purpose of defining it to be an abstract description of "that which created the universe." For the moment, I am not saying that this is the same as the Judeo/Christian notion of G-d. I could have just as easily called it "Fred" and, just for the sake of clarification (and comedy), as well as not wanting to step on anyone's religious toes, I will do so from here on in.

How did Fred create the universe? I haven't the slightest clue, nor do I honestly believe that humans will ever have the capacity in our primate brains to get that clue. We haven't even been able to decide how we create ideas, so how are we supposed to understand how Fred created the universe? If we can't describe how Fred created the universe, then maybe we can ask why Fred created the universe. Once again, Fred's motivations are, to my belief, unknowable and beside the point. At this point in time, I haven't even stated that Fred is a sentient, thinking being. Perhaps the universe was created by accident, or as a side effect of some other act. If this is the case, then the motivations behind the universe's creation are quite depressing. Maybe Fred did not make a conscious decision to create the universe, in fact; maybe Fred does not even possess consciousness. What if Fred doesn't? Ahhh, this leads us down a much more productive thought path. We can now begin looking at Fred's personal attributes and seeing what consequences they might have for the universe and its creation.

One important question is whether Fred is physical, or beyond the physical world. This question brings us full circle to my other question regarding mentally ill individuals. If one is not adhering to consensus reality, and altering brain chemicals can bring that individual back to consensus; is there really anything other than chemicals and physical "stuff" to the world and our perceptions of it? This is a very good question, one that can also be traced back to Fred. Is Fred simply a cocktail of chemicals and other physical "billiard balls" or is Fred something else; something beyond the "veil" of our physical world? Before addressing this question, I would like to return to whether or not Fred is sentient. It would seem, at least according to my definition of sentience, that it doesn't matter if something is physical or ethereal to be sentient, it would simply have to be a Source. Recall that a Source creates Ideas which manifest themselves as Symbols. Ideas themselves seem to be manifestly non-physical, so could Fred also be an Idea, or like an Idea?

There are several possibilities here. If non-sentient, then Fred is not a Source and therefore, incapable of creating Ideas and must be reduced merely to a symbol. I don't think that I'm the only one uncomfortable with that definition; therefore I will go ahead and assume Fred to be sentient and a Source. With that out of the way, is Fred physical or non-physical? Well, as I said before, a Source may be either physical or non-physical. However, if Fred is physical, then we can begin another stapler-like regression forming: what created Fred? What created Fred's creator? And, since we can assume the universe to be all-encompassing (or any combination of parallel universes thereof); we end up with a paradox. Barring creation from nothing, you get an infinite regression where there must be a creator to create a creator to create a creator to create a creator… This is unacceptable.

If non-physical, then Fred is like an idea, but an idea whose antecedent has to be the Fred Source. This is similar to the former case of Fred being physical. In other words, Fred had to create Fred, but also had to already exist to create Fred. Fred is the non-physical creation of himself, the cause and the effect. This cycle is unbreakable, unknowable and within it lays the nature of the universe itself. Fred is that cycle, the infinity, the paradox. Fred is the unknowable, the unfathomable and the unnamable.

Ideas Symbols and Sources

I do believe however, that Fred created the universe with a single idea. Fred is an unknowable, paradoxical idea-like thing from which sprang our universe and our existence. How this idea differs from the ideas that you and I have everyday is not clear, however I don't believe them to be very different at all. I have always believed that it is not the work of philosophers to answer life's questions, but merely to pose them. So I end this chapter, leaving the reader to ponder one great question. If the unnamable can create the universe with a single idea, then what power lies in our own ability to form ideas? Think about it.

The Meaning of Life

I know that at least a small portion of you may have picked this work up just for the sake of this chapter. The meaning of life is a very hot topic. Some of you, no doubt, just wanted to see what I professed to know on the subject before rejecting it wholesale and throwing it away. Others may just be curious and want to hear other opinions on the matter before forming one of their own. Finally, the most gullible of the group may think that I actually have some kind of insight into the true meaning of life and want to get a piece of the action (to the latter group, buy 20 more copies and in the twentieth one, the true meaning will be revealed to you, snicker, snicker).

Well, to spare everyone the suspense, I'll say right now that, no, I do not have the true meaning of life anywhere in this book. You will not find it anywhere. There. Those of you in the first group, feel free to throw this away right now. Those in the other two groups may wonder why this chapter is still going on and why I haven't gone on to the next. Well the answer to that is fairly simple. I happen to believe that there is no "true" meaning of life that supersedes all others. I believe that each individual has a different meaning of life that can, and usually does, change over time as that individual evolves. It's like a time-varying DNA. I think it is improper to ask someone "what is *the* meaning of life," and one should rather ask "what is *your* meaning of life."

That said, again, what justification is there for this chapter's continued existence? Well, as almost everyone has heard at some point or another from a high school guidance counselor when choosing a career, "it's just as important to know what you don't want to be as it is to know what you do want to be." In the same line as that, I would like to discuss one thing which I believe is decidedly *not* the meaning of life, even though a lot of pop culture sells it as such. As you might have guessed, this thing is money, or more generally, materialism.

We live in a culture that embraces the capitalist economic system. This is both a good and a bad thing. It is basically the most effective and prosperous economic system the world has ever known. It is responsible for the greatest gift America has given to the world, an attitude that always approaches a problem the same way, by saying "I can do it." The free market economy has enabled everyone to work for their piece of the pie based on their own strength, giving endless possibilities to the masses. This is the core of the American Dream, a wonderful and unprecedented perception in the world. But at the same time it creates an almost pathological avarice among most citizens. We here in the US live in the wealthiest society ever seen on this Earth. We have so many opportunities to pursue wealth that we can't choose between all of them. This is the birthplace of true rags to riches stories, sacred tales of self-made men who worked their way to the top producing and receiving untold amounts of wealth.

However, the dark side to this story is the psychology that it has created. People chase wealth and money, as they always have, but with an abandon bordering on obsession. People begin to see money and things as the only possible pathway to happiness, to the exclusion of everything else in their lives; family, friends, hobbies and leisure. People work tirelessly to make more and more money so they can buy more and more things that they don't need. Welcome to the consumerist culture that is modern America.

To what end must we chase this chimera of happiness? The consumerist drive is similar to that of an addict. There is an overwhelming drive to buy, buy, buy, buy; to make more and to have more with no end in sight. It is a compulsion. This is the point at which materialism has supplanted any reasonable meaning of life and taken over.

But wait a minute; didn't I just say that meaning of life is an individual thing? Who am I to say that material obsession is a non-valid meaning for life? Simple. As stated in the Love chapter, we are working under the Aristotelian assumption that the ultimate end of all human action is happiness. A materialist is no more capable of achieving happiness through consuming than a crack addict is capable of achieving ultimate happiness by smoking crack. The happiness is fleeting and ultimately unfulfilling. Therefore, any self-defeating addiction such as this cannot be a valid meaning of life for that person.

I am not saying that all material consumption is bad. This is patently obvious (see <u>Atlas Shrugged</u> by Ayn Rand). It is only when material consumption becomes the prime focus of one's life and takes on that individual's "meaning" moniker does is get out of hand. I think that this is fairly intuitive to most people. What is not intuitive to many people is that materialism takes on many forms besides shopping sprees.

We have all known people in our lives that just can't stop sleeping around (see the Sex chapter). Aside from all of the problems presented in the Sex chapter, those that have tons and tons of indiscriminate sex with many different people basically exhibit the same compulsion as someone who collects insane amounts of shoes. They are compelled to collect independent of need or use; whether physical objects, like shoes, or abstract objects, like sexual conquests. In fact, the word "conquest" itself gives insight into the meaning behind the meaning of its usage.

It does not simply indicate overcoming some struggle or obstacle toward luring a potential mate to bed, either through charm, con or blackmail. As made I made abundantly clear in the Sex chapter, I strictly believe that love is the one and only acceptable requirement for sex. Therefore, the thought of duping someone into sex, or even just using charm with no deeper feeling attached to lower the target's defenses is repugnant enough to me. However, the meaning behind the meaning is what is more repugnant to me, to the point of being anathema. The word "conquest" changes the person into an object.

For all the millennia leading up to our "advanced" civilization, this concept of lowering a human being to something subhuman has been responsible for more violent and sociopathic atrocities than any other. Before committing a huge atrocity, such as genocide, it is always the case that the group facing extermination has been dehumanized in the eyes of those committing the atrocity. Reducing a human being to an object makes one capable of anything. Obviously, sleeping around indiscriminately is not the same as genocide; however I do believe that the basic mindset of someone bent on collecting "sexual conquests" is more or less the same as someone bent on committing genocide. That is that both have selectively reduced a specific group of human beings to objects.

This person has not only divorced his emotions from his body and mind, but he is also working under a faulty meaning of life. This further supports my contention that those engaging in tons of indiscriminate sex with many partners are some of the most misguided, even deranged, people in the world. While this problem usually seems to be more prevalent among men, there are plenty of females out there sleeping with every guy they can find. Each and every one of them, male and female, are going about trying to find happiness and meaning in the wrong way. They are chasing a phantom of meaning that lures an individual on and on, with no end in sight; like a carrot being dangled at the end of a string.

I say this because I believe that each of us has to have a *valid* meaning of life around which to shape our lives. Again by valid, I mean something that leads us toward a fulfilling happiness as a result of our actions. The lost, the disenfranchised and the bereft are often said to be lacking a direction for their lives. Basically this means that they are either working under an invalid meaning or they don't have a meaning at all. It is important that people always reevaluate their own specific meaning and hold it close in everything they do. It doesn't mean that it won't change over time, but one must always look in his heart to see the true meaning of his life. It was Socrates that said "an unexamined life is not worth living."

Meanings will be different for different people, but it should always lead to a long-term fulfilling happiness. The trouble is, how can one tell if a path will lead to such an undefined concept? Quite simply, you can't. You can't peer into a crystal ball and magically tell what path will lead to long-term fulfillment; but you usually can tell which paths won't. Compulsive shopping and indiscriminate sex are just two examples of actions that definitely fit the category of "invalid life meanings." Most people that engage in these activities even know that, but they lack the vision to see that even temporarily adhering to such a meaningless value system will have lasting effects.

The key is to simply stay away from the invalid life meanings, and through trial and error, work to find meanings that do fulfill. That's not to say that the meaning won't change over time, it certainly will, but it's the effort and the searching that matters. By that same token, no one should ever fall into the pit of indecision and allow himself to abdicate his right to choose meaning. That is just as bad, if not worse, than choosing an invalid life meaning.

Choosing a path can be very frightening. "What if I make a mistake?" and "How can I possibly know what is a good choice and

Philosophy Junk Food

what is a bad choice?" are common worries. It is natural to feel that way. However, it should never take over one's life and terrify an individual into inaction. One should take comfort in the fact that choices are rarely irrevocable and that nobody knows where their path is going to take them from the outset. If we did, where would be the fun in life? The best advice I've ever received on the subject is from my Mom. In any given situation "all you can ever hope for is to do your best and hope for the best." Usually things work out as long as you keep this attitude. If things don't work out the way you expect, oh well, just get back on the horse and try again. We have been given the greatest gift anyone can ever hope for; the chance to chase our dreams. In chasing them, the most important thing is not to give up.

That being said, I would like to share a few things that are small pieces of the puzzle, you can think of them as "mini-meanings" of life:

Star gazing on a cool clear night away from city lights

Waking up, seeing dew on the grass and smelling that indescribable smell of morning

Marveling at the complexity of how our own bodies work

Scoring the go-ahead goal in the 84th minute of a crucial match

Talking and laughing with your friends, about anything from the Big Picture to how the ladies are treatin' ya

Cruising on the freeway, jamming to your favorite song

Making sweet, respectful love to your loved one

Having a dirty, un-kosher fuck with your loved one

The Meaning of Life

Watching a sunset

A nice cold beer on a hot day

Accomplishing a long-time goal after a lot of hard work

Touring a foreign country, especially with your best friends

Landing a great job

Enjoying the holidays with your family

Graduating

Having an experience that makes you look at life in a new light

Partying your ass off until dawn

Realizing that you don't have all the answers, and feeling good about it

Learning a new language

Playing a song that you wrote in front of an appreciative crowd

The first kiss of what you know will become an important relationship

Staring out into the ocean and feeling that cosmic sense of insignificance

Being in the mountains and feeling connected to the past, before suburban sprawl took over our national landscape

Seeing your favorite band live in concert

Realizing that, no matter where it came from, life is the greatest gift of all and that no matter what happens, good or bad, you should enjoy it and be thankful because it could be taken at any time and it won't last forever

Philosophy Junk Food

Women and Men

What is the longest war in history? If you said the Hundred Years War between England and France of the 14th and 15th centuries you would be sorely mistaken. The longest war, of course, is the Battle of the Sexes. Although it's not clear who or what began this war, it has certainly escalated to Biblical proportions (especially when you think about that messy snake and apple business). These details mean little, however, when looking at the current state of affairs. Both sides have become very aggressive and are hell-bent on total victory, no quarter given. Recruits are snapped up early in life and given training so pervasive in their everyday lives that, once fully conscripted, combatants have the army's goals woven into the very fabric of their being. It is as if they are brainwashed from childhood to fight to the bitter end…

This may sound a little apocalyptic and over-dramatic, but hey, give me a little poetic license here. Besides, is it really that different from the true nature of our education in the opposite sex? By design, this view is also a little ridiculous because, G-d help me, I can't help but think it's ridiculous anytime I ever hear anyone refer to male-female interaction as some kind of war of aggression. So, as a preamble, I say to all the Feminists, Masculists, Neo-Feminists, Nouveau-Men, and other such nonsense: **Get a grip. Chill out. 99% of everything you believe about the "War between Men and Women" is in your head.**

I say 99% because there are still a few issues between men and women that have some merit in a logical sense. There is still a small income gap between men and women and we still have yet to see a female US President. The matrimonial and family courts also have a bias against men; if don't believe me look at divorce judgment statistics and you'll be singing a different tune in minutes. In this country, these are really the only true disparities still affecting men and women. However, this will not last as women already have a disproportionately high enrollment in institutes of higher learning and their presence continues to increase in all traditionally male walks of life. On the male side, the kind of injustice experienced in the court system cannot last long in a society that values fairness as much as ours.

The female disparity is a throwback to a time when women were treated as second-class citizens rather than equals to men as far as productivity and potential to do well in society. The "old-school" attitudes toward women were as pretty objects and breeding stock. These, quite frankly, disgust me. However, we have come a long way from that and I believe the remaining gaps are meager compared to the chasm faced by women 100 years ago. However, "awareness" about these perceived gaps continues to be beaten, dead horse-like, by bullshit activist groups trying to convince the thinking, voting public that their cause deserves special treatment (start writing your hate mail). Whininess and greediness cross all demographics and whenever an activist group smells blood in the water (the possibility for: handouts in the form of reparations, reparations for reparations, legislation that gives them advantages, legislation that disadvantages opponents etc.) they move in for the kill (convincing voters and legislators that opportunity gaps in the form of discrimination are far, far more serious than they truly are). Naturally these activist groups receive vast amounts support from the groups they supposedly represent because, like whininess and greediness, another trait that crosses all demographics is the willingness to trade in self-respect and moral principles for free shit (keep that hate mail coming).

The activist groups that support men are no better. The bias in the family court system came into existence primarily because of myths about males' inferior ability to raise children. These myths come from the same era and are in the same tradition as the myths regarding females' inability to equal males' productive value. Overblown statistics about fathers' propensity for child abuse didn't help either. The fact of the matter is, this will not last forever, but still we have activist groups raising hell about the inequity of life for all men.

As far as I'm concerned, what the particular activist group is supporting makes not one bit of difference to me. I could care less about the opinion of some rage-driven, invective-spewing quasi-psycho yelling that women have unequal access to purchasing Mike and Ike's as compared to men; or that men are being screwed over by the system because women have so many options when it comes to tampons and men have none. The heart of the matter is that the groups themselves don't really care about the issues they claim to care about. The people who have the organizational capability to pull something like a large-scale protest off are not stupid; and they realize better than anyone that a large-scale protest is a great way to get money and special favors from elected officials. They use the issue as a smoke-screen to peddle influence and obtain what they really want, power. The rank and file of these movements are just tools to get their leaders the power they want.

The major fallacy these groups make lies in the underlying assumption they make about the nature of men and women. You see, they supposedly advocate "total equality" because they assume that men and women are exactly the same in essence. The thing that these bullshit activist groups are unwilling to reveal is that (hold on to your hats) **MEN AND WOMEN ARE NOT EXACTLY THE SAME.** I know this is a mind-blowing concept, but bear with me. This kind of statement can easily land me categorized as a misogynist or some kind of anti-progressive throwback to the days of pre-suffrage. This couldn't be further from the truth. In fact, that kind of vile invective is the kind that is most likely to be spewed by the aforementioned bullshit activist groups. Such passionately irrational and combative responses absolutely reek of ulterior motives and have no place in civilized discourse.

It is common for one to fall back on an emotional declaration when one has no rebuttal based on logic. This tactic is used to a T by most of these activist groups. If a dissenter offers a logical counterpoint to a statement of the group, they will immediately brand him a "misogynist/misandrist" in an attempt to destroy his credibility. This is a classic false dilemma logical fallacy. You paint the opposition as being a fearsome, anti-social nutcase and then present the audience with a choice of either "choosing our side or choosing the anti-social nutcase."

In order to make a reasonable analysis of the situation, I believe we need to make one major postulate on which to predicate all statements. That postulate is that societal and biological imperatives are independent of one another. This is where many supposedly logical arguments about female/male gender roles break down. We attempt to sweep all defining characteristics of men and women under the rug. We take the very essence of what it means to be male or female, quite possibly the most important part of an individual's self identity, and we toss it out the window like so much trash. We operate under the assumption that we are all the same. If ever there was a crazier notion to be uttered, I have yet to find it.

This statement is categorically **NOT TRUE** and (discounting any major change in biology or some evolutionary jump) **IT NEVER WILL BE.** The differences between men and women are more than skin deep. Research has shown that women's and men's brains are structured differently than one another. The way we talk, the way we listen, the way we relate to others, the way we act and the way we think are totally different. Don't get me wrong here; I'm not saying that all male/female differences can be attributed to nature over nurture. There definitely are influences in society that mold a young girl or a young boy to have certain expectations and perceived duties. But these are right now in a state of flux, the end result of which no one can know. Let's take a quick look back to when all this change started happening.

Throughout The Enlightenment and more progressive eras of recent history, traditional societal expectations began to come under some scrutiny. Not last on the list was the issue of gender roles. How should women and men act? What is their role in a family? What is their role as far as a career? And, of course, what about the sex?!?! As we humans are apt to do, we began experimenting to try and see what works best.

All of this came to a head in the United States about 90 years ago when everyone looked around and said "Holy crap! We're supposed to be the archetype for all freedom and democracy and 52% of our population can't even vote!!!!!" Women's suffrage came and was a triumph (amazing to me it took us that long to do it). Soon after that, the walls for women that traditionally stood began crumbling like a month-old Bundt cake. Women entered the workplace, they started going to college in droves, and they started running for office. Sexual barriers fell just as readily. Pre-marital sex became commonplace, pornography appeared in the mainstream, marriage was no longer a prison to truly unhappy couples, and single bachelorettes became (and are still in the process of becoming) respected and accepted.

Philosophy Junk Food

This was the Big One as far as gender equality. The totalitarian regime of Victorian decorum had finally fallen. Men and women were free to be the masters of their own destiny. As stated before, there were/are still some social barriers, mostly for women with a few for men, of which the remaining ones will be gone very soon.

In step the bullshit activist groups, keeping in mind that these groups know their points to be pure rubbish; they just want the power. You've got groups saying that sex is an inherently degrading act; you've got groups saying that boys with competitive tendencies need anger management; you've got groups condemning young women for wearing revealing clothing to attract men; you've got opposing groups each saying that the other the opposite gender is unfit to raise children or abusive; it goes on and on. In each and every one of these cases, the groups want some kind of payoff, be it legislation supporting their cause, preferential treatment or just outright reparations. In nearly all cases (disclaimer: "nearly") there are two fallacies at work here.

Fallacy number one involves generalizing specific cases to a whole gender. This is the case with the abuse and unfit parenting cases. Abusive tendencies and an inability to parent correctly cross gender and racial boundaries. Attempting to attribute these things to any one group is preposterous. Think back to early human evolution; if all men/women were abusive/incapable of raising children, would the human race have survived up to now? NO! We would have all been victims of spousicide or infanticide long before McDonald's opened its doors.

Fallacy number two involves, as stated previously, the incorrect assumption that men and women are the same. This comes in two flavors, the type that bone-headedly denies simple biology, and those that deny behavior patterns hardwired into us eons ago. The claim that sex is inherently degrading is obviously of the first flavor. How stupid can you get? If you have a problem with the way our bodies were designed take it up with G-d. I can't believe the idiots that preach that shit even get the time of day. How can one judge the way that our bodies have evolved to function, let alone blame the other gender on the problem!? It would be the same as me saying that the way that our stomachs digest food is a vile, horrifying degradation of food's rights. How can we sit by and watch as poor, pathetic Cheetos that never even had a chance are being corroded by acid and ground up into mush? Something must be done about it! Sheesh.

The second flavor is tricky, because it crosses into that grey area of nature versus nurture. The young woman dressing provocatively and the competitive little boys fall into this category. Trying to prevent a young woman from dressing provocatively is a harkening back to Victorian repression. Young women and men are supposed to attract one another, it's a biological imperative. Young women are just using the freedom given to them by permissive societal rules to accomplish that goal. The desire to attract potential mates is an ingrained behavior that transcends any higher-level social programming. It is one of the most basic, and one of the most important, behavioral rituals performed by anyone. How do we expect to propagate our genes if we don't attract a mate?

The same thing is true in the case of the little boys. The little boy acting competitive on the baseball field is supposed to do that. Competitiveness is natural for men; it's hardwired into their brains. Men must show strength and vitality to each other and to women, it is analogous to a woman dressing provocatively in that it is a show of their prowess to other men and a show of their virility to women. The little boys acting out on a sports field are learning how to create that image of fertility through play in formative years. In fact, both of the actions of the women and the actions of the men are essential parts of creating this image of fertility. Without that image, it would be much more difficult to perpetuate your genes to the next generation. The lack of this image is usually accompanied by a profound appreciation for Star Trek.

The behavior patterns that men and women follow were developed over millennia of natural selection and, for all intents and purposes, have been optimized for success in life. Now, there are some that would claim that the modern landscape of human society has made these behavior patterns obsolete. I'm not in a position to argue that point one way or another, but I will say this: if it is true, it will become apparent over time. Major social changes happen naturally over time; they are not legislated or artificially imposed on society by activist groups looking for handouts.

Women and Men

So what's the next step? Can we salvage our civilization? Will we ever be able to successfully bridge that chasm separating the two halves and become one complete unified species? People have been trying for most of civilized history, but just on a smaller than global scale. This guerilla tactic to infiltrate the opposite side is called "marriage." The combatants are either scared to death and draft dodging (bachelor/ettes), going through boot camp (serious relationship), down in the trenches trying not to get shell shocked (hitched) or grizzly veterans regaling everyone around them with tales about how hellish the war is (divorced).

War analogies aside, marriage certainly isn't easy (never having been married myself, I'm sure those of you that are/have been are going "Oh you have NO idea"), but it has certainly gotten a lot tougher in recent years. There is a great deal of buzz about a perceived "marriage crisis" gripping the country. Statistics assail us claiming that the divorce rate in this country is more than 50%. We hear anecdotal tales of people being taken to the cleaners by angry ex-spouses in divorce court; about people saying the wrong thing at the wrong time to the judge and never being able to see their children again; about owing more than 100% of their income in alimony. It's downright scary. To my knowledge, never has such a supposedly joyous occasion been infused with such fear and anxiety. It's like worrying that some years after your graduation, your alma mater would decide that it didn't like you, divorce you, and then take away

Philosophy Junk Food

your degree, your house and the salary from the job it got you. That's pretty harsh dudes and dudettes.

So what gives? Are we just much less mature than our great-grandparents? Why can't we make marriage work the same what they did? I think the root cause is, as it is for most endemic social problems, quite complicated. I do not believe that we are fundamentally less mature than any other previous generation. I also believe that it's a copout to assume that's the reason. My opinion is as follows: along with new freedoms and options comes increased opportunity for discontentment. The more choices we have, the more apt we are to fall victim to a syndrome so old there's even an aphorism associated with it: "The grass is always greener on the other side of the fence." Basically, people become discontented with their partner because, once committed to that person, suddenly all the other options walking by you on the street, at the gym and on the elevator seem much more attractive than they did before. Before long, you start to think that maybe you made a huge mistake. Maybe there is the natural 2-year sexual cool down when your dopamine (the "in-love" hormone) levels start returning to normal. Maybe you start arguing with your spouse over things you never argued about before. Maybe nothing significant happens; you just start to feel antsy and bored. In any case, our newfound sexual and social permissiveness has removed the stigma on divorce and, voila! you're calling your lawyer.

I realize this is very oversimplified and I'm going to expand on it now. Obviously in the above scenario, the primary marriage must already be somewhat rocky if either or both are considering being unfaithful or divorcing. I'm not one of those people that says "once you're married you have to stay married *no matter what*." Far from it. I believe that the removal of divorce stigma is a great thing. There are definitely marriages that are beyond help and should be ended. If abuse is involved, of course divorce is warranted; that's a no-brainer. However, my criticism today is that people are far too trigger-happy when it comes to divorce. Pundits say that since divorce is a now multi-million dollar business, barriers to obtaining one keep falling one right after another, giving people easy access. This is no excuse, however. In my opinion, once married, a couple has a responsibility to do everything possible to save their marriage before taking steps toward ending it. If a couple is taking that responsibility seriously, it shouldn't matter how easy getting divorced is.

Attitudes about relationships and marriage have changed a lot in the past century, but not enough to account for the jump in the divorce rate. I think that, although both have probably gone up, the divorce rate has risen disproportionately to the number of unhappy/borderline marriages. Again, this is simply due to the destigmatization of divorce as an institution. 75 years ago, there were plenty of unhappy marriages, but because of attitudes about divorce, many people stayed married rather than risk the wrath of their parents, friends and churches. Now, divorce is as common as tax loopholes and people just can't get enough of it. Which brings me to my real point to this rant: just because you can get a divorce, doesn't mean you should, as least not right away. People should understand that they have a responsibility, not only to themselves and their spouse, but to their children (if there are any) and even society in general to do whatever it takes to save a marriage before heading down to the Law Offices of Cohen, Cohen and Schwartz.

Why am I so vehement about saving marriage? Simple. It is possibly the most important societal construct developed by humanity. Remember back in the Love chapter I said that love is a bond developed by nature to bring couples closer together in order to raise their children correctly? In the Sex chapter I said that a child needs both a mother and a father figure in order to develop optimally. Quite simply, if we get rid of marriage and allow single parenting to become the rule, I believe we are going to decline very quickly. I believe that, overall, society will be more poorly adjusted, and less capable of functioning at the levels it would have had it remained majority two parent. Don't think I'm taking a shot at single parents or children from one parent families. There are millions of one parent families that do just great and have kids that grow up wonderfully. I'm just saying that the continued development of society will be aided if two parent households dominate. This is why people also have a societal responsibility to try and make marriages work, especially if they have children.

This may sound like diet advice from a fat person, seeing as I've never been married. However, I do have the best role models on the subject, my parents. They have been happily married for 32 years and they have certainly taught me that a long-term loving commitment with the right person can be more satisfying than a cold Coors Light on a summer afternoon in Arizona.

I know this is counter to all that pop culture is trying to sell us, what with endless sexual freedom being extolled as the greatest virtue of all. They offer a world where everyone sleeps with everyone else in utopian harmony, free of all emotional entanglements. They show marriage as a prison, a sexual wasteland, a place where has-beens that can no longer pick up 21 year olds at bars go to wait for death to release them, the good days of life far behind. Invariably, they use this image attached to an advertisement, using the glamorous images of promiscuity in an attempt to sell you something you don't need. The ones that fall for it have had the wool pulled over their eyes. It's a sham; a dirty, shameful fraud. What they don't tell you is that, with the right person, marriage and monogamy are true freedom, and that promiscuity is the prison. That's what my parents taught me, not through words, but through their own actions of loving one another, and my sister and I.

As a qualifier, and to avoid supporting any psycho right-wing family values groups, I will say that everyone has a right to live as they want to. If promiscuity is your game, then by all means, play it and enjoy it (safely). However, I don't believe that it gives the depth, satisfaction and happiness of a long-term monogamous relationship with someone you truly love and respect. Say, speaking of happiness...

Happiness and Sadness

Happiness and Sadness

Isn't happiness a bitch? It's vindictive, sneaky and downright difficult to find. Finding happiness is kind of like an Easter egg hunt throughout all of Manhattan, where half the eggs are rotten. I know I've talked at some length about people's ergons and how happiness is the ultimate end of all human action. After that, you may be thinking to yourself, "OK, I'm supposed to find happiness (as if that weren't about as obvious as an elephant hiding behind a telephone pole) but where do I start looking and what am I even looking for?!?" As Shakespeare would say, "aye there's the rub." Where do we find happiness? What do we do when we don't even know what will or won't make us happy? How do we set goals that are realistic and work for us in our lives?

These are all valid and important questions to ask. However, in regards to the subject of happiness, they are also completely irrelevant. These types of questions pertain to the subject of meaning, not of happiness. As outlined in the Meaning chapter, each person has an individual meaning they have to find on their own and which acts like a guiding light in their life. It is a blueprint of the general direction their life needs to take. It's not a roadmap to happiness because, you see, happiness is not a destination, it's a journey.

Many people run into trouble with this. They think things like, "Once I get that big house, I'll be happy," or "If I could just find a great new girl/boyfriend, I'll be happy," or "Once I get promoted, I'll be happy," or any other such statements that everyone says at some point in their life. This kind of thinking is self-defeating and ultimately, leads to more and more unhappiness. If one gets stuck in this kind of thought loop, then what you get is a positive feedback loop of unhappiness. The more things/goals/achievements that are obtained and fail to bring about the expected happiness, the more things/goals/achievements are craved. When eventually achieved, these things/goals/achievements don't bring the expected happiness and yet *more* are sought. On and on we go in a death spiral of unfulfilled expectations and unhappiness.

It is true that graduating from high school or college or starting a new relationship with someone special can definitely make you happy. In fact, these are some of the things that make life worth living. However, it is a subtle difference in attitude that determines whether the experience is ultimately positive or negative. The happiness comes not from the expectation that graduating will somehow remedy a state of unhappiness. If one has this expectation, he will undoubtedly be let down and disappointed in the outcome. One must be contented with the journey, the effort and the opportunity, only then can one fully appreciate the accomplishment.

The same goes for relationships. We've all heard the aphorism "you must be happy by yourself before you're ready for a relationship." While I don't usually go for that kind of pop-psychology bullshit, there is a kernel of truth in it. You can't expect a relationship, or anything else for that matter, to single-handedly solve your depression.

Philosophy Junk Food

One tendency that is becoming very prevalent in today's society is the prescription of antidepressants. Before I pigeon-hole myself into some unthinking cult that condemns antidepressants in all cases (Scientologists) let me say that I think they are a wondrous invention. For people that truly have brain chemical imbalances these are a life-saving invention and a gift from modern medical science. Used properly, this family of medications can work miracles. However, I do believe that they are rampantly over-prescribed. This is a manifestation of our quick and dirty, instant gratification approach to all things; drive-thru happiness. Doctors want to maximize their profit margin by having as many patients as possible. It is much easier to give a patient a prescription for SSRI's in a 10 minute consultation once a month than to actually counsel a patient properly. Proper counseling takes 3-6 times as long and will net you approximately the same amount of money as the 10 minute consultation. Being a practical, profit minded individual, the doctor takes the obvious choice.

It is not completely the fault of the doctor, however. The patient is just as much to blame. If a person can get their brakes serviced 15 minutes, why should a doctor's visit take any longer? This is the 21st century; anything can be fixed by taking a pill once a day dammit. Instead of taking the time to explore the causes of their depression, people just take these brain-altering medications to treat the symptoms. Feeling blue? These pills will return anyone to the pre-approved, industry standard mood level. No further effort required on the part of the patient. Orwellian eh?

I contend that in the majority of all cases in which antidepressants were prescribed, they were unnecessary. I believe that most of the people have been cruelly duped by a medical community that sees our lives only as a string of chemicals and not as a whole. Again, these medications are a life-saver in some cases, but most of the time the doctors are selling snake-oil. In the snake-oil cases, individual counseling (without drugs) and a change of perspective on the part of the patient is what is truly needed. This does take more effort on both sides, but it treats the cause and not just the symptoms.

True, lasting happiness must be internally motivated. You must have the right attitude about your life in any case or condition, be that single, engaged, married, divorced, paraplegic, terminally ill, skinny, fat or Geraldo Rivera. That attitude, not drugs or any other outside stimulus, is what will save you from yourself and allow you to be contented. What form that attitude takes differs from person to person.

For some people, religion gives them the right attitude. For others, it's some inner vision to strive for. The point is this: none of these things originate from outside the subject. They are internally conceived and the subjects' actions are motivated such that they don't deviate from what they know holds true to their vision. This way, achieving a great goal is a wonderful bonus, but it is not *required* for happiness. Since an internal vision of happiness is being followed, the subject is happy all throughout the journey. In so many words, the key to happiness is inner peace with one's actions and the consequences of those actions, subjectively positive or negative (man that's some more pop-psychology bullshit, I apologize).

Coincident with this, happiness is truly a choice on the part of the individual. I believe, through the great wisdom of my father, that any occurrence in anyone's life can ultimately be interpreted as having a positive effect. To find that positive effect is a matter of outlook and a matter of attitude, both of which require a conscious choice on the part of the individual. In my estimation, one can basically choose to allow events to cause long-term unhappiness, or choose to not let them. It is natural for people to feel short-term unhappiness after a painful event, but it is a choice whether a person allows that event to vanquish him. You can either lie down and wallow in the cellar of unhappiness, or you can rise from the ashes like the Phoenix and reclaim your rightful place as a joyous being full of potential and life.

It is easy to fall back on cheap cynicism and shoot down these life-affirming statements (life-affirmation in America is almost as unfashionable as being a white male nowadays). I believe, and always have, that cynicism is a poorly conceived disguise for insecurity, fear and inability to cope with a situation. Cynicism toward one's prospect for happiness, or even the existence and capacity for happiness itself, is actually a cry for help. It's someone saying, "I'm so miserable, and I want so badly to be happy, but I just don't know how! I'm afraid of what it will take! I've been unhappy for so long, that I'm afraid of what will happen to me if I am happy! What the fuck am I supposed to do?!??!" But instead of showing that vulnerability to a world that he perceives as cold and indifferent, he dresses it up with statements about how happiness is a fraud, a joke, a fabrication by those that don't understand the *true* nature of the world.

On somewhat of an aside, it's funny to me how prevalent this attitude seems to be amongst urban dwellers and so-called progressives, and how scarce it is among simple rural folk. It seems ironic that those who proclaim to have superior knowledge about the ways of the world are so lost when it comes to the single most important thing in life; learning to be contented with one's own existence. From personal experience, it would seem that the people "popular society" condemns as unsophisticated hicks have a far more developed notion about how to live a fulfilling life than those who make up the "popular society."

Again, I would be attacked by cynicism: "What's so great about living a fulfilling life? That's an outdated notion. You should know that fulfillment is impossible and even if it were possible, why should I want it?" Those who claim that a fulfilling life is either not possible or undesirable have become so skilled at self-deception, they might also believe that they are actually not human, but Komodo dragon. It's obvious, even to the speaker, that such statements are lies. It's just pointless posturing about how their life is more meaningless than his neighbor or his cousin, because, for some goddamn reason, meaninglessness and suffering are very fashionable right now (I wish I knew why, must have something to do with residual effects from the Seattle grunge movement). Everybody wants to jump onto the nihilism bandwagon and prove that, by G-d, their life is the *most meaningless of all*. If the speaker actually believed the tripe he's saying, he wouldn't be announcing it to every passerby on the street, he'd be sitting in his room holding a revolver and thinking about whether the great-beyond has more fulfillment than this life.

These types like to quote existential philosophers (especially Nietzsche, usually out of context) and make drastic (il)logical jumps from general statements of metaphysics. These jumps always end up in this same place; life is, of course, meaningless. First off, if you already know your destination, and you aren't interested in using logical arguments, you can basically take any statement, make enough (false) conclusions and end up where you want to be (life is meaningless). Example: "I will prove life's meaninglessness by the fact that many potatoes come from Idaho! Potatoes are grown by farmers! Farming is difficult! Difficulty is innate to human existence! Therefore, human existence is meaningless! Take that you motherfucking optimists!" (Speaker lights a cigarette and continues reading The Birth of Tragedy in original German despite not knowing a single German word)

Secondly, these people have either never actually read these philosophers, or they just got to the place in the book they wanted (life is meaningless) and stopped reading. If they had continued, they would have found that Nietzsche warns that nihilism is the *improper* direction to take when analyzing how his ideas affect your own life. In fact, Nietzsche believed that the ideal human (the übermensch) should live life joyously and go through life with supreme purpose toward his ultimate goal. Nietzsche recognizes the "void" of human existence; that is, he saw that life can be interpreted as meaningless when considering the big questions of existence. The übermensch needs to recognize the void for what it is and accept it to become a complete individual. He does not allow the void to conquer him and cast him into infinite despair and inaction; he masters it and moves on with determination. From there, he is able to create his own meaning and his own happiness, free of any societal metanarrative.

From this view, the nihilists are an un-evolved and un-enlightened group. They have faced the void and instead of joyously reveling in the freedom of their own existence and accepting their birthright to make their own way through the world, they sit down and cry like cowards about how happiness and meaning are cruel lies. It is human nature to only want to do as much as you absolutely have to; laziness seems to be a genetic trait native to the species. So, naturally, these people refuse to make the necessary effort to create their own meaning, choose happiness, and live a joyously productive life.

Philosophy Junk Food

That is why Nietzsche's übermensch is a figure of great courage and conviction. He does not take the coward's route of giving up once a roadblock is thrown up. Instead, he plows forward with the knowledge that this life is **his** and no one else's; and he will use that life to the absolute fullest by making a place and meaning for himself through his own efforts. Backing down and giving up the opportunity to make that meaning is a huge cop-out and the largest act of cowardice a person can know. You can see now why I have no respect for cynics or whiny nihilists; they casually throw away the gift of life with pitiful cries about the injustice of the world and its lack of meaning. Own up to the world, stop whining and choose life and happiness. You'll not only make yourself happier, you'll make me happier because I'll no longer have to listen to your bitching.

A Partridge in a Pear Tree

Philosophy Junk Food

A Partridge in a Pear Tree (aka: Priorities and Success)

The last chapter is upon us, and not a moment too soon! Take comfort in the fact that it took many times longer to write this than to read it. Before I set off into my final rant, I would like to thoroughly thank you, the reader, for your time and attention. Creating something from the heart and soul is not an easy task, and there is nothing more gratifying than getting to share it with someone else. The one thing that I hope this work does for you is get you to think and to make opinions of your own on whatever subjects you feel passionate about. Whether you loved this work or hated it, the purpose here was to show my own personal point of view on several issues facing our society today. I would love to think that I encouraged some people out there to think about those issues and form their own opinions. Don't take my word; what the hell do I know anyway? I'm just a snot-nosed, entitlement generation punk. That said, thank you again.

Where would you like to be in five years? Nearly all of us have heard this question at some point in their lives, whether it be in a job interview, from a family member or from an in-law skeptical of future employment possibilities. It's a tough question. It presents the perfect amount of time to throw you off the track; just far enough in the future to make things hazy, but not so far that you can make up completely cliché abstract nonsense like "in a 30-year fixed rate with

2.3 kids, 1.7 pets, 1.2 soccer teams, a 2.1 car garage and a white picket fence." It's tough to make any kind of definite determination of goals that far ahead of time without relying on those abstract, universally acceptable signs of a successful and productive life. However, the difficulty in answering lies not in the question, but in us.

The problem here is that people usually have a very clear set of priorities for the short term (I would like to get a second date with Stacy because she has very nice jugs) and for the very long term (the 2.3 kids crap) but they have no practical way of bridging them together. What are we to do in the intervening time between scoring with Stacy and settling down with Stacy in a 4,000 square foot suburban home? Somewhere along the line, there is a discontinuity in the priorities. If a person's priorities could be represented by a road map, the short term plan leads to a certain point then stops at a canyon; on the other side of the canyon, the road picks up again and continues. People know that they want to get to the second segment of the road (their long term goals) but the gap over the canyon between the first and the second segment has no bridge. The bridge is not there because it's never been built.

Many, if not most, people float through life only living by their short term set of priorities (for my age demographic this usually consists of getting drunk/high and having sex) and expect the long term priorities to magically take over at some point and cause their life to fall into place. They ignore the chasm between line segments and expect, with no extra effort, to transport to the long-term results

Philosophy Junk Food

they envisioned in the second line segment. Granted, everyone has heard anecdotal evidence of someone that this works out for. We hear of some slacker who was a friend of a friend in high school that hits it big in an extravagant series of extremely lucky events. For some reason, our culture, at present, seems very preoccupied with these stories of improbable arrivals at the top (American Idol). These stories are, without a doubt, amazing simply because of the odds that have to be beaten. It plays off a common fantasy of being lifted from mediocrity to the upper crust through little or no effort (Great Expectations).

The fact is, for the vast majority that follows this path; things don't usually end up exactly the way they hoped. Getting to the top of anything, be it entertainment, business, technology or academia, takes a lot of planning, prioritizing and, most importantly, hard work. These people have had high expectations of reaching some far off destination of "success" without any clear way of getting there. The road map of their priorities has had a canyon with no bridge since they started driving. The people following this path never realized that you have to make sure the road is complete before you can even begin driving. The only way from point A to point B is a continuous road. By the time they realize this, it's too late to reach the far-off point B of their ideal life and they must take a detour.

This can lead to widespread dissatisfaction with a life that might otherwise be considered perfectly acceptable. A typical situation is an individual at the tender age of 27 (or something) with a well paying corporate job, a spouse and kids. This individual will be so miserable and feel so trapped that a crack den would appear more appealing. Long ago, he didn't take the time to make sure the bridge between short term and long term goals was built, so he ended up being forced to take a different route. Even though the destination at which he has arrived is, by most accounts, a great life, he feels cheated. He feels as though he never had a chance to live the life he wanted and that the life he has now was not chosen by him but for him.

He does not take the time to consider all that he has to be thankful for at the moment. He is too preoccupied with the lost opportunity to arrive at the fantasy world of his long term goals on the other side of the canyon. What he does not realize is that he never had a chance to live that life because he never built the bridge at the very beginning. If he is miserable, he has no one but himself to blame. His life is not miserable at all. In fact, by most measures, it is downright idyllic.

The solution to this quandary is the same regardless of the individual's phase of life. That solution is the willful creation of a universal set of life priorities. There can be no disconnection where he has one set of priorities at one point in his life and another for later on. This is a nice idea in theory (like Communism) but in practice it is impossible to tell when the transition from one stage of priorities to another actually arrives. The building of a universal set of priorities for each step of life corresponds to building the bridge across the canyon. In fact, a good set of priorities is not like just one bridge, it's like filling the entire canyon with concrete. That way the future that allows freedom to go wherever he wants.

Since the solution is the same in all cases, the only thing that matters is at what point the solution is applied. This is what will determine the future from any given point in an individual's life. For example, let's look at our hypothetical 27 year-old. Let's assume a ground state priority set, as stated before, of getting drunk/high and having sex. He is basically floating through life, passive to most things. He enjoys life well enough for the time being, riding the dopamine high of self-medication and casual sex.

However, once we fast forward we can see that he's gone through three large, obvious, life changes in the mean time. He got a corporate job, he got married and he had kids (not necessarily in that order). In any case, since he was floating through life at the time, he made these big decisions on the spur of moment, on his best knowledge at the time. The most important thing that he did not do, however, was rearrange his priorities to integrate these huge changes into the mosaic of his life. He wakes up one day, as though from a coma, and finds himself in a job, with a wife and kids that he feels as though he didn't choose to have. His priorities still dictate drunken sex and a floating, generally irresponsible lifestyle.

Our subject here, let's call him Jim, has fallen prey to priority inertia. At some point, preferably before making this first of his three big decisions, he needed desperately to come up with a more complete picture of his priorities for the entirety of his life. This does not mean a detailed list of planned major life events and associated dates, it only means that he had to look critically at his life and decide what he wanted out of it. He needed to consciously decide what his course of action should be at a given time, and consider the consequences of what it would mean to the whole of his existence. Instead of deciding to get married at the spur of the moment, he needed a vision of his priorities first, and then he could decide how being married fit into that vision.

The one major variable here is the point in his life at which he comes up with this "priority roadmap." Let's say he critically looks at his life and finds that what he actually wants is to become a rock star. It is not impossible to make this vision a reality at any point in time, but it would be much easier before he gets settled into all these responsibilities. If he makes this determination while still in his formative years, he can direct his actions inexorably toward his final goal across the canyon of being a rock star. He can plan out each step and make sure that he is on the correct path. He can still have drunken sex if he chooses to, but he is no longer a floater as long as he continues to work toward that singular goal. If he works hard enough, stays focused and gets a little lucky; he may cross the canyon into the land he always envisioned.

The later he makes the determination, the more effort and the greater the sacrifice is required on his part to accomplish his goal. All is not lost, but what lies ahead is difficult. If me makes his priorities after his big, life-altering decisions, he must weigh what he's already got versus what his "true" ambitions are and how much it will cost him to achieve those ambitions.

This is where the order in which those life changes occur actually does become important. Let us assume the most common scenario: he gets a corporate job, gets married and has kids. I realize that this is a large supposition nowadays but for the sake of simplicity, let's go ahead. If he has the rock star epiphany after he has gotten his job at Sell-You-Useless-Shit Inc., but before he's gotten married, it is a relatively simple task to quit and begin spending his time writing bad music. It does take a modicum of courage even to quit a job you don't like, however, so while it's simple, it may not necessarily be easy. He still has to stick his neck out a little bit in order to follow his dream.

If he waits even longer and reorders his priorities after he gets married, the task becomes more complex and more difficult. What will his wife say when he says that he is no longer going to be receiving a steady paycheck? What will she think of her husband touring the country, hanging out in bars and having women's underwear thrown at him on stage? Will the marriage survive? Now he faces the problem of not only having to quit a job, but also possibly get a divorce if everything does not go according to plan. At this point, he has to stick his neck uncomfortably far to follow his dream.

Finally, if he waits even longer and reorders his priorities after he has children, the task is ridiculously complex and nearly impossible. The priority has now become a selfishly immoral thing simply because of the timing. It is basically incompatible with the life he has already chosen. The children depend on him for their lives and he no longer has the luxury of capriciously throwing away a stable career to serve his individual whim. Had he reordered his priorities back before he allowed himself to sleepwalk through his life choices, it would not have been selfish, simply ambitious. However, because he refused to stand up and look at his life priorities from the start, he now has to choose between giving up on what he believes to be his true calling, and betraying the children he brought into the world to an unstable emotional and financial future.

The single best option available to Jim is to stop looking to the past, be a mensch, accept the responsibilities before him and reorder his priorities according to their requirements. Instead of looking at his family as a burden holding him down, he can look at them as a gift to be cherished. This is not making the best of a bad situation; this is changing his point of view and creating a life mission to live up to and thrive in (see Happiness and Sadness).

Simply because he can't run off and be a rock star, doesn't mean that he is doomed to a mediocre and unfulfilling life, he simply needs to look critically at what he has, what his responsibilities are and what he wants. After doing that, he can make a "priority roadmap" that works with his current situation and makes for a rich satisfying life. For instance, instead of becoming a rock star, he could enter the music business on a more white-collar basis. If he doesn't have the necessary experience, he can go back to school. This is a viable option that doesn't sacrifice his wife and children's stability and happiness. Self-interest is a virtue; he'll be a happier person and a better husband and father if he improves his own life. Even if he feels like he didn't choose his life, he *did* choose to have a family, and he has to live up to that responsibility.

I don't know if this problem of apathy and prioritization inertia is unique to my generation, but it is certainly endemic to it. I think the cause is a combination of fear and lack of responsibility (see Responsibility). We dislike taking responsibility for anything, so perhaps taking responsibility for our own lives is simply too big of a chore. It would put us out on a limb that we don't like, a position where we only have ourselves to blame if we fail. In lieu of facing this, we avoid making priorities at all.

The fear aspect is an even bigger problem, however. This fear comes in many different flavors: fear of the unknown, fear of failure and, my personal favorite, fear of success. These fears all basically come from the uncertainty about one's own ability to make and carry out a plan of action. This is the ultimate impotence of my generation. We have grown up in a McSociety that values consumerism, excess and social isolation; it is only natural that our ideas of success naturally revolve around those values. We are driven to make the maximum possible money (not a bad thing in itself as long as the task you're doing to make the money is a true passion for you), consume the maximum amount possible and "protect" that which you have acquired from a cruel and indifferent society.

Too often I've seen, not just in my generation but especially amongst Baby Boomers, that any reordering of priorities often strictly involves becoming "successful" in this way. Not becoming "successful" shows that you are directionless, confused or just plain lazy. This by no means states that I am against being ambitious about making money and acquiring toys that you want. On the contrary, making money off of an activity that you love is a great joy. My personal view of the American Dream is overcoming odds to choose a path that you are truly passionate about and making money while enjoying your life for every wonderful second it brings.

However, the love and passion for one's work has been taken out of the modern view of success. We are driven solely by what will get us the most in the shortest amount of time, hence the widespread envy of Paris Hilton amongst the younger crowd. She doesn't have any skills to speak of, she doesn't work, and she doesn't really do much of anything outside of partying. Yet she has everything our current code of success dictates, i.e. a glamorous life of money, fame, fabulous celebrity parties, and an endless line of beautiful potential bed-buddies. Therefore, to many impressionable young and not-so-young people, she is the pinnacle of a successful and fulfilled person.

My view of Paris Hilton is of a tragic person who had all the luxuries of life handed to her with no effort on her part. She has never and will never taste the sweet nectar of reward for a true effort toward a goal and, therefore, is about as unsuccessful as she can get. There has never been a desire or a drive because there was never a need for either. She is the exemplification of a floater. She doesn't

Philosophy Junk Food

need to analyze her priorities because there is never a life-choice requiring her to do so. She has no true passion, no true goals and no true values outside of the next big Hollywood bash. The heart and soul of a fulfilling life are absent in her endeavors, so she can never hope to attain any real satisfaction from her existence. Tragic indeed.

A truly successful person can look at his priorities and have an idea where he wants to be at any time. These priorities are a plastic, constantly changing thing because, as mentioned in the Meaning chapter, a life must be constantly under examination. He will set goals, work toward them, sometimes he will fail, sometimes he will succeed, but he will always be *successful* because of the effort. When he fails, he won't become unhappy because, as the Happiness chapter mentions, happiness is a choice and a matter of perspective. Most importantly, he will feel the supreme joy of being alive to experience it; the joy of freedom to make those priorities and those choices; the joy of the effort; the joy of feeling pain from failure and the sweetness of achievement.

It's exactly like a soccer match. Soccer is the perfect microcosm of life in its beauty and simplicity. The full gamut of emotions is run a hundred times in each match. The goal is clear, the rules are simple. You must work as a team, but each member relies on his individual skill to further his cause. There are great accomplishments that go unnoticed, and big mistakes that directly affect the outcome, but all that is eclipsed by the sheer, youthful, unadulterated joy felt by just being able to participate. Victory can be intoxicatingly euphoric and defeat can be agonizingly miserable, but the satisfaction felt from the effort, victorious or not, is the true meaning of the game. That is what it means to succeed in soccer as in life. If you don't know soccer, go learn it. You'll learn more about life than anyone could ever tell you.

People were meant to succeed in this way and you can start any time. It only takes the smallest effort on your part to take that first step. Set your priorities and work toward them. Work hard; struggle and, while you may fail, don't forget to think about the freedom of just being able to pursue that struggle. Understand that the freedom you have is a glorious gift unequaled in the universe. Remember that you are a luminous being meant to find joy in each and every thing around you. That is our birthright. (That's about as mystical and preachy as I can get, but this is the end of the book so I'm a little emotional)

"The sun will set tonight on all the lonely dreamers, only to rise again so we can start it over." The words of Brock Lindow, my favorite metal philosopher, illuminate the true meaning of success. Everyone has dreams and goals, even if they're buried deep within a rockslide of cynicism, apathy and fear. But each of us has the power to overcome difficulties and take chances in order to fulfill those dreams. The struggle and the joy derived from it, as well as the joy derived from the outcome are true measures of success. Hardships may come, but never give up, life and happiness are much too important for that. In the immortal words of my sister, "Don't let the bastards get you down."

Philosophy Junk Food

Again, thank you for giving me the time it took to read this. I appreciate that you would let me rent out a few precious hours of your life; I hope it affected you in a positive way. I don't profess to be an expert on anything, but it's nice to have another person to share my ideas with, even if the exchange is far away and not face to face. It falls to you, the reader, to interpret these ideas however you wish. If I sound like an asshole sometimes, I promise I'm not really an asshole in person. In fact, if you are ever out in Denver or Boulder and see me at a bar, I promise I'll buy you a beer… provided you have a copy of the book with you to redeem as a credit (just kidding). My final words: remember to always love with abandon, make mistakes, don't hold grudges, and reach for the stars in everything you do. Again in the words of Brock Lindow, "everything will be alright, even if the city ignites."

Appendix: Suggested Reading, Watching and Listening

Reading Material:

Atlas Shrugged by Ayn Rand

Slaughterhouse-Five by Kurt Vonnegut

The Brothers Karamazov by Fyodor Dostoevsky

The Mote in God's Eye by Larry Niven and Jerry Pournelle

The Birth of Tragedy by Friedrich Nietzsche

Thus Spake Zarathustra by Friedrich Nietzsche

Nicomachean Ethics by Aristotle

Being and Nothingness by Jean-Paul Sartre

"Living Like Weasels" by Annie Dillard

The Death of Ivan Ilyich by Leo Tolstoy

The Foundation Series by Isaac Asimov

To Kill a Mockingbird by Harper Lee

A Separate Peace by John Knowles

The Turn of the Screw by Henry James

Hamlet by William Shakespeare

The Guiness Book of World Records

The Culture of Narcissism: American Life in An Age of Diminishing Expectations by Christopher Lasch

Burmese Days by George Orwell

Anything by Jacques Derrida relating to Deconstructionism

Fear and Trembling by Søren Kierkegaard

Catcher in the Rye by J.D. Salinger

The Great Gadsby by F. Scott Fitzgerald

Catch-22 by Joseph Heller

Candide by Voltaire

Hitchhiker's Guide to the Galaxy by Douglas Adams

We by Yevgeny Zamyatin

The Grapes of Wrath by John Steinbeck

War and Peace by Leo Tolstoy

Anything by Tony Hillerman

Visual Material:

The Star Wars Series

I ♥ Huckabees

American Beauty

The World's Fastest Indian

Dogma

The Big Lebowski

Donnie Darko

Jerry Maguire

Good Will Hunting

Rushmore

High Fidelity

Swingers

The Sixth Sense

Rudy

The Boondock Saints

Run Lola Run

Philosophy Junk Food

Northern Exposure

Star Trek (any movie or series)

Listening Material:

36 Crazyfists

A

Incubus (Anything but "Crow Left of the Murder")

Taproot

Flaw

311

Bob Marley

Chevelle

The Gin Blossoms

The Postal Service/Death Cab for Cutie

Modest Mouse

Gorillaz

The Format

The Refreshments/Roger Clyne and the Peacemakers

They Might Be Giants

Collective Soul

Matisyahu

Santana (The Older Stuff)

Brandenburg Concerto No. 4-6 (Bach)

Silverchair

Bullet for my Valentine

Aceyalone

Del tha Funkee Homosapien

Fanfare for the Common Man/Appalachian Spring/Rodeo (Copeland)

Weezer (Blue Album or Pinkerton only)

At the Drive-In

40th Symphony/Eine kleine Nachtmusik (Mozart)

Blur

Stone Temple Pilots

The Mars Volta

Skin Flick

Acknowledgements

First and foremost let me thank my family, my parents Judy and Larry, my sister Rachel, brother-in-law Scott and my beautiful girlfriend Kate. I would also like to thank the posse: Rob, Mat, Kaveh, Singer Dave, Lincoln, Jeff, Winny, Marc, Ziad, Crazy Brian, Tom, Ryburn, Erin, Derrick, Derek, Skin Flick, Kendra, Stephanie, Luke, Travis, Nate, Brett and basically anyone else putting positive energy into the world. Without you this never would have been possible.

I would like to not thank anyone trying to suppress the human spirit in any way, anywhere, at any time. You are the ones responsible for most of the world's ills.

About the Author

David Schuster was born in Albuquerque, New Mexico in 1981, smack in the middle of the MTV Generation. He has a bachelor's degree in physics Magna Cum Laude from the University of Arizona, a master's degree in physics from the University of Miami and, as of the printing of this, was working on his Ph.D in astrophysics from the University of Denver. He is a card-carrying member of Phi Beta Kappa, the Libertarian party and Sam's Army (if you don't know that one, learn the world's game for crying out loud!). He is a 20 year veteran of the soccer field as a player and a 2 year veteran as a coach. He is adept at performing voodoo love spells, as evidenced by his snagging a hot sorority girl in Arizona (that's you Kate) in spite of also being a die-hard Trekkie. He plays bass guitar, recorded an album with his rock band, Skin Flick, and was even briefly signed to a record contract (no shit!). He is also an avid skier, yo-yoer, juggler and gamer. He has never done underwater basket-weaving but he is willing to try. His life ambition is to become a Jedi.

Philosophy Junk Food

Philosophy Junk Food

www.ingramcontent.com/pod-product-compliance
Lightning Source LLC
Chambersburg PA
CBHW051805040426
42446CB00007B/527